Augusto Floriano Jaccaci

On the Trail of Don Quixote

Being a Record of Rambles in the Ancient Province of La Mancha

Augusto Floriano Jaccaci

On the Trail of Don Quixote
Being a Record of Rambles in the Ancient Province of La Mancha

ISBN/EAN: 9783744694469

Printed in Europe, USA, Canada, Australia, Japan

Cover: Foto ©ninafisch / pixelio.de

More available books at **www.hansebooks.com**

ON THE TRAIL
OF
Don Quixote

Being a Record of Rambles in the
Ancient Province of La Mancha

BY

AUGUST F. JACCACI

ILLUSTRATED BY

DANIEL VIERGE

NEW YORK
CHARLES SCRIBNER'S SONS
MDCCCXCVI

To
William C. Brownell

PREFACE

THIS book is the natural outgrowth of a friendship between artist and author — the one a Spaniard, the other familiar from youth with Spain, and both lovers of the book wherein are recounted the adventures of the good Knight and of his faithful Squire. The writer had always felt that the illustrations of Cervantes's immortal romance should be the crowning achievement of Vierge's career, and it was primarily for the purpose of giving Vierge the opportunities of gathering the documents from life and nature necessary for such an undertaking that the two friends had for years projected a journey through La Mancha, for it is incredible how few changes have taken place in the home of the hero since the days of his wanderings. The customs, the character, the manner of dress, and the speech of its inhabitants, have remained practically unchanged, and of its landmarks Cervantes has made such vivid pictures that one finds it easy to identify them.

Preface

Through unexpected circumstances the artist had to go alone, and less than a year after the author followed minutely his friend's itinerary. As it is, pictorially and in words, this book is "un livre de bonne foy," a simple record of notes and impressions from nature. The text telling of wheat-harvesting and midsummer sunshine; the pictures depicting grape-gathering, wine-making, and the lowering gray skies of Autumn.

It is safe to let speak for themselves the pictures of that master draughtsman who, in remaining scrupulously true to facts, has the power to endow them with the dramatic feeling, the nervous charm, of his artistic personality.

The writer felt, more profoundly than he could express in words, how, in such a community, the remnants and voices of the past form an essential part of the living present. He wished above all that he could have made his rambling notes ring with more of his keen delight and appreciation of active, open-air life in a rarely varied and picturesque region happily as yet despised by the tourist.

November, 1896.   A. F. J.

CONTENTS

CHAPTER I

ON THE ROAD TO ARGAMASILLA

PAGE

Madrid—Ciudad Real—Manzanares—A Bodega—The Postal Carriage—Argamasilla de Alba, . . . 1

CHAPTER II

ARGAMASILLA

Gregorio—The Parador del Carmen—Posada Life—The Popular Idea of Don Quixote—The Men—The Women—Religious Feeling—Landowner and Tenant—The Casa de Medrano—Don Rodrigo de Pacheco—Cervantes's Birthplace—The Priest—The Guadiana, ... 15

CHAPTER III

THE CAVE OF MONTESINOS

Ezechiel's Cart—The Guardias Civiles—The Fulling-Mills—Ruidera—Lunch—Mule and Muleteer—Osa de Monteil—A Goatherd—The Cave—The Lagoons of Ruidera, ... 61

Contents

CHAPTER IV

MONTEIL

PAGE

El Cortijo de San Pedro—The Hermitage of Saelices—A Homicide—The Lagoons—The Castle of Rochafrida—The Taciturn Shepherds—Villahermosa—The Castle of Monteil—Pedro the Cruel and Henry of Trastamara—The Old Romances—The Return Journey—Hunting—Another Legacy of the Moors, ... 85

CHAPTER V

EL TOBOSO

The Plain of La Mancha—The Venta de Quesada—The Royal Highway—Herencia—The Feast of St. James—The Church—Guitarists—Alcázar de San Juan—The Wind Mills—Campo de Crijitano—Siesta—Toboso—A Model Inn—The Fanatic Proprietor—A Quinteria, ... 111

CHAPTER VI

THE MORENA

Ezechiel's Adieux—Valdepeñas—Almuradiel—Old José—The Sierra—Viso del Marques—Casa Teresa—The Fiesta—The Bull Fight—An Open-air Theatre—Excursion to a Mountain Garden—Los Molinos, . 173

Contents

CHAPTER VII

VENTA DE CARDENAS

PAGE

The Royal Highway—Typical Mountain Scenery—Venta de Cardenas—Apprentice Toreros—A Family of Bohemian Fakirs—Despeñaperros—Andalusia, . 215

LIST OF ILLUSTRATIONS

	Page
The guest-room at the Casa Teresa, El Viso. The holy images on the walls, the little statuette of Our Lady on the fine old chest of drawers are such as one finds in all nice houses of La Mancha,	Frontispiece
Lunch-time in a bodega. Manzanares. The peasant laborers who find employment during the wine-making season come from all parts of La Mancha. To save the little money they make, they sleep in the doorways of the houses, and live almost exclusively on "garbanzos" and coarse black bread,	2
Head of a blind mendicant,	3
A Tobosan woman cart-pedler on market-day,	5
The court-yard of a chalk mill at Manzanares,	7
A postal carriage on the run from the station of Argamasilla to the pueblo,	9
A peasant of Puerto Lapice peddling fruit in a street of Alcázar de San Juan,	10
A "galena," a sort of farm wagon, in general use in the Castilles,	13
Gregorio, the "amo" of the Parador del Carmen,	14
A woman of Monteil,	17

List of Illustrations

	Page
Muleteers in the posada, Argamasilla. Their scant and typical costume, short trousers, hemp sandals, tied with ropes round their legs, kerchiefs round their heads, and "fajas" (belts), is the same all the year round, except that in winter a coat, or "capóte," is added,	*19*
The little plaza behind the church at Argamasilla. In the street opening on the row of houses shown in the drawing is situated the Casa de Medrano,	*20*
Scene in the posada stables, Argamasilla,	*21*
Weighing grapes in the court-yard of the posada, Argamasilla,	*22*
Tobosan pedler of puchéros (glazed wares),	*23*
Gregorio's wife buying from a street-pedler (one from the plain of Monteil, judging from his furry cap),	*25*
One of the rare good times of the women. The "ama" visiting a friend. The scene is the hall or passageway behind the street-door, which is used among the village people as living-room, parlor, etc.,	*27*
The kitchen of the Parador del Carmen,	*28*
The posada of Argamasilla at grape-harvest time, when the grapes are carried from the "galenas" into the big stone vats where the wine is to be made,	*30*
A street scene in Osa de Monteil, the woman knitting in a chair before her doorstep, perfectly undisturbed by the pigs there squatting about,	*33*

List of Illustrations

	Page
The entrance of the cellar which was Cervantes's prison in the court-yard of the Casa Medrano,	34
The cellar prison, showing the old door (It is now used as a sort of store-room for jars of wine, etc.),	35
Don Rodrigo de Pacheco. A sketch taken from the head of the painting at Argamasilla,	37
"His favorite chair in the barber's shop." A portrait of the priest spoken of in the story; the same shaving-basin, primitive old lamp, of like model and fashioned by hand as in Cervantes's time. The fine matting on the floor shows this barber's shop to be the "Salon Café," where all the notables of the pueblo gather,	39
"Feminine curiosity." The posada of Argamasilla. The screen of wood-work through which the woman looks is essentially Moorish,	40
The priest's niece looking down from her balcony (Argamasilla),	41
"Feminine curiosity." A woman, rigged for work, her heavy outside skirt gathered up round her hips, interrupts her scrubbing to look at the passer-by—a rare enough occurrence in the usually quiet streets of Argamasilla,	43
The plaza of Argamasilla on market-day. An autumn scene when the air is sharp in spite of the sun. The first peasant merchant in the foreground wears a "cdpa," the second is bundled up in a "capóte." The church shows in the background,	45

List of Illustrations

	Page
A scene between a pedler and a house-keeper, showing the interior of a house of Toboso—one of the oldest and most picturesque houses in La Mancha,	46
A woman looking at peasant pedler's stock of pumpkins—Alcázar de San Juan,	49
Dance at the posada, Argamasilla. No refreshments but water are served at such dances. The orchestra is composed of guitars and a violin, but the guests join from time to time in a song,	50
A scene in the posada, Argamasilla,	53
A street scene at Almuradiel, showing a lot of freshly gathered peppers hung up to dry,	54
Ploughing in the highlands, between Monteil and Villahermosa,	57
Ezechiel's cart at the gate of the posada, Argamasilla,	59
A Ruidera street scene, showing the ungainly and heavy costume of the woman, skirts pulled up on the hips, revealing the trousers worn underneath. The two ruffians in the foreground are types of shiftless individuals who loaf as a regular mode of life. The young woman in light clothes, with a broom in her hand, is the newly married "ama" of the house where artist and author found shelter,	62
Ezechiel's cart, which is built on the same principle as the Sicilian and Maltese carts, and the "araba," the only vehicle known in Northern Africa,	64
The road to the Fulling Mills,	65

List of Illustrations

	Page
A characteristic bit of scenery on the way to Ruidera,	66
"Arrieros" on the road skirting the lagoons of Ruidera,	68
An incident of the artist's journey where, before the Cortijo de San Pedro, the swollen lagoons had overflowed the road,	70
A street in Monteil. The furry cap of the figure in the foreground was the Manchegan headgear in Cervantes's time,	71
A woman of Ruidera,	72
Another street scene of Ruidera,	75
The entrance to the Cave of Montesinos. There is another, which is some two hundred feet to the right, but being well-like, it is impracticable,	76
Episode of the artist's journey: Near the cave,	77
Episode of the artist's journey: The cart-driver urging him to depart from a posada when he and the family had hardly sat down to their meal,	78
A bit of Monteil,	79
Type of goatherd, sketched near Villahermosa,	80
The lagoon of La Colgada, near the cave of Montesinos, the deepest and largest of all the lagoons of Ruidera,	81
The edge of a lagoon,	83
The ruined interior of the hermitage of Saelices,	86
The entrance to the hermitage of Saelices,	89
Skirting the lagoon near the Cortijo de San Pedro,	90
An upper valley of the Guadiana,	91
Shepherds' huts, sketched on the road to Villahermosa,	92

List of Illustrations

	Page
Shepherds in the cañon-like bed of the winter torrent, between the valley of the Guadiana and Villahermosa,	93
The Castle of Pedro the Cruel, at Monteil, as first seen on coming from Villahermosa (the village of Monteil being hidden behind the hill),	96
The Castle of Pedro the Cruel, from a street in Monteil,	97
A typical afternoon scene in a street of Monteil. The woman beckoning with her hand in the foreground is a pedler of lottery tickets,	99
Approaching Villahermosa,	101
The Castle of Pedro the Cruel, from a street in Monteil,	102
An episode of the artist's journey: Arguing with the driver of the cart, who for some reason does not wish to start, while the artist's friends see that the proper provisions are packed in the baskets for the journey,	104
Street scene at Villahermosa: The old duenna in the foreground signs herself devoutly in passing before the holy image of the Madonna, dressed up like a doll, and set up on a little altar-like affair against the wall of a house. A pair of crutches on one side of the statue, some wax feet on the other, show the gratitude of people cured by the miraculous intercession of this particular image. Three of the horribly maimed mendicants, that one sees only in Spain, are lying on the sidewalk under the statue,	105

List of Illustrations

	Page
The entrance to Villahermosa. The barber's shop in front,	*107*
Sleeping quarters of the artist in a private house of Villahermosa,	*108*
The dance at Herencia. The semi-civilized dress of the men is typical of Herencia, one of the most prosperous towns of the province of Ciudad Real,	*112*
The Royal Highway between Madrid and Seville,	*115, 117*
A solitary mendicant on the Royal Highway,	*118*
Pedler selling his stock of cotton cloths at auction in a street of Herencia,	*121*
The plaza at Herencia. The fonda spoken of in the text is on the right-hand side of the picture. A boy, following the old custom, which was a universal one until of late, runs to kiss the hand of a priest he meets,	*122*
A corner of the court-yard in the fonda of Alcázar de San Juan, where the grapes ready for wine-making are heaped up,	*124*
The façade of the fonda at Alcázar de San Juan,	*125*
A bit of Alcázar de San Juan,	*126*
On the outskirts of Alcázar de San Juan, the beginning of the road to Crijitano, a water-pedler in the foreground, behind him a characteristic wayside sanctuary,	*128*
Ajutamiento (City Hall), Alcázar de San Juan,	*130*
In the Ajutamiento Tower, Alcázar de San Juan,	*131*
The wind-mills of Crijitano, as seen from the distance,	*132*
One of the ancient wind-mills of Crijitano,	*135*

List of Illustrations

	Page
A typical bit of scenery at the mills of Crijitano,	136
An episode of the artist's journey: On approaching Crijitano,	137
Sketched in one of the upper streets of Crijitano, a typical arriero in the foreground,	139
Episode of the artist's journey: The entrance in Campo de Crijitano, behind his escort of Guardias Civiles,	141
The distribution of bread to mendicants, a daily occurrence of Campo de Crijitano (In accordance with a legacy left over a hundred years ago to a church by which a certain amount of money has to be expended in giving bread to the sick, cripples, or very aged poor of the locality),	142
Façade of a house at Campo de Crijitano, dating back to the Moorish occupation. All its details and the lower porch, supported by columns, are distinctively Moorish,	143
A corner of the plaza, Campo de Crijitano, the church's principal entrance on the left,	144
View of Toboso from the plain, with the big, squat church-tower spoken of in "Don Quixote,"	146
The entrance of the posada at Toboso,	147
A street of Toboso, a pedler selling honey in the foreground,	150
A street of Toboso,	151
The plaza at Toboso, the church on the left,	152
An episode of the artist's journey: Guardias Civiles, in search of a robber, making an investigation,	155

List of Illustrations

	Page
A bit in Toboso,	157
The kitchen of the posada in Toboso,	159
The well in the court-yard of the "posada" at Toboso,	160
Maria, one of the daughters of the "amo" of the posada, Toboso,	163
Posada, Toboso: Detail of staircase, with charmingly turned baluster,	165
Posada, Toboso: Entrance to the wine-cellar,	166
Juana, the other daughter of the "amo" of the posada, Toboso,	167
Picking saffron flowers. As in Arab countries the women do the work, the man being a sort of overseer,	169
The laborers' lunch at harvest-time in a "quintería,"	171
The Sierra Morena, from the station of Almuradiel,	174
Doña Teresa washing,	175
The Sierra Morena, from the plateau between Almuradiel and Viso,	177
Episode of the artist's journey: Arrival of the traveller's cavalcade in view of Almuradiel,	179
A bit of El Viso,	183
Miguel de Cervantes y Saavedra. The traditional face which is held in Spain to be that of Cervantes, although there is no evidence to prove it, and, on the contrary, strong evidence to disprove it (It is doubtful if any contemporary portrait of Cervantes exists),	185

List of Illustrations

	Page
A corner of the patio, Casa Teresa, El Viso,	186
In a Manchegan boys' school,	188
Episode of the artist's journey: Scene in the Venta de Cardenas,	191
Episode of the artist's journey: The departure of the artist's party from El Viso for an excursion to the mountain-garden spoken of in the text,	192
The Sierra Morena, from the plateau behind El Viso,	195
A characteristic bit of the central massif of the Sierra Morena, near the Venta de Cardenas,	196
Lunch in the little garden of the mountain,	197
Episodes of the artist's journey: Depicting the incidents which befel his party on the way to and from Los Molinos,	198, 201, 203, 204, 206
Type of "arriero" on the road,	208
The peak of the Panero, one of the bleak mountains encircling Los Molinos,	209
Episode of the artist's journey: Departure from Santa Cruz de la Mudela. The mule in the foreground has the characteristic pack-saddle used in the mountain country,	216
Episode of the artist's journey: A scene at the Venta de Cardenas. The Maritornes presiding over the cooking. In the background a set of dangerous-looking "arrieros,"	220, 221
An episode of the artist's journey: Alarmed at the roughness of manners and bad looks of a band of "arrieros" which they found at the Venta de Car-	

List of Illustrations

	Page
denas, the members of the party decided to spend the night in the open near the lonely building of the station, where, under the watch of their two Guardias Civiles, they felt more secure than in the "venta,"	222
The famished toreros, watching the stranger eating,	224
The toreros,	225
Episode of the artist's journey: Night scene at the Venta de Cardenas. The conference between the guardias and the little party, when a hasty departure was decided upon,	226
The fakirs coming into the Venta de Cardenas,	228
The fakirs' siesta in the Venta de Cardenas. In the foreground a hand waving the Manchegan fly flap,	229
Night scene in a popular resort of Seville,	231
Los Organos in Despeñaperros. The railway on the other side of the gorge midway up the mountain,	233
A detail of Los Organos,	234
The " arriero" singing a " malagueña,"	237

I

On the Road to Argamasilla

Dinner-Time in the Bodega—Manzanares.

On the Road to Argamasilla

IT was night in July, and I was bowling along toward the same dreary plains of La Mancha, that were the scene of my youthful tramps. Friends had just warned me most earnestly not to venture into that country of rough, half-savage folk unless I secured an escort of police from whose sight there must be no wandering, "for," they added, "the navaja [the knife] is handy down there;" and the manner of their speech was tragic. But then they were Spaniards, and must regard things in the national way—that is, to revile natives of other provinces than their own, and more particularly the inhabitants of unlovely La Mancha, the most backward region of Spain.

With occasional sleepy glances into the future (I was stretched on the long seat of an empty carriage), mingled a shifting consciousness of the adieux of the people of the

On the Road to Argamasilla

Madrid hostelry—doubly cordial in expectation of a promised reward for the safe-keeping of the luggage left with them—of the drive through the narrow streets to the station looking all the way at the Madrilenes, out for the freshness of the evening. They little knew how glad I was to be among them again and how delightful was to me the animated spectacle of their streets. I remember distinctly in a little plaza, over whose miserable pavements my rickety carriage went bumping in unexpected and distressing fashion, the candle-lighted booth, frail affair of wood and paper, where I stopped to buy delicious oranges for next to a smile from a swarthy woman dressed in rags, her hair a-tangle but with the condescending manners of a princess.

In the station, stiff and gloomy, a porter, loaded with a tiny package, my one change of linen, preceded me with dignified steps and throwing open the door of a first-class carriage with a bang that re-echoed all over the place seemed thus to apprise onlookers of the fact that here was indeed a lordly person, one who, in spite of his diminutive luggage, could afford the luxury of the

On the Road to Argamasilla

best. There are always lookers-on at the departure of a train in Spain. Travelling is such an unusual and risky proceeding that family and friends feel called upon to testify, by their presence, their concern in the perilous undertaking.  No doubt prayers are indulged in for weeks previously, letters are sent beforehand informing all of the fateful event. Even after the great day has come and gone, how can the household or the little circle of friends at the café resume the even tenor of its way without hearty expressions of concern and wishes that all may be well with the adventurous one?

What a contrast was Ciudad Real, the worthy, because so very poor, capital of La Mancha ·("Imperial and the Seat of the God of Smiles," as Cervantes termed it), to the bustling New York I had left but twelve days before. In the early morning,

On the Road to Argamasilla

pure and fresh, the crystalline magnificence of the pale green sky brought out in strong relief the insignificance of the little town and its rambling low houses. The bareness of the whitewashed walls was made more emphatic here and there by some iron-screened window, or a door bristling with nails and ornate locks and hinges. All was strangely quiet in the long, narrow, unpaved street which led into the heart of the little town and the same oppression of silence so striking in Arab cities falls upon the traveller. Indeed La Mancha is Moorish, country and people. The Moors have left their thumbmark, the traces of their long domination, on the aspect of the towns and the physiognomy of the people, not less than on the character and temperament of the inhabitants and their social and domestic relations.

It was Arab hospitality of the best kind that awaited me as I knocked, a stranger at an unseemly hour, at the house of the father of Carlos, the friend I had just left in Paris. Everything was done to make Carlos's friend feel at home, and my new acquaintances proved so much more helpful than our national representatives in Madrid had been

On the Road to Argamasilla

that by ten o'clock I was able to continue my journey, having in my possession an order from the governor of the province that I should be furnished with an escort of mounted police wherever I might wish during my travels.

The train crawled along in an African landscape. The plain, with vegetation the color of its soil, stretched out in supreme desolation under the blue sky filled with the cruel majesty of the noonday sun. No settlement, no houses, nor any signs of life enlivened this torrid desert till on the path running beside the track some brown specks came bobbing up and down toward us — a characteristic

On the Road to Argamasilla

group; ahead the man on donkey-back, his legs dangling, his head thrown back and a glimmer at his open lips. Following on foot came the woman, with long, swinging strides that sent her heavy skirts flying in rhythmical and recurring folds. A young donkey wandered behind his dam in his own sweet, fitful fashion, all ready to scamper in case of pursuit.

It was a melancholy contrast of sexes, which the woman did not realize. More melancholy perhaps was the contrast between the man and the beast he bestrode, which looked as if each weary step would be its last. Spanish owners of beasts of burden, knowing the very last notch of fatigue and hunger their poor drudges can reach, keep them relentlessly there, thus getting the most work for the least expense. But they shrewdly allow the young ones to grow in freedom and comparative plenty so as to be strong for the ordeal to come.

The wayfarers had nearly passed, the man singing at the top of his voice and looking straight before him, when the woman turned her eagle's profile with a sharp motion and gave us a long blinking glance. In all prob-

On the Road to Argamasilla

ability she had never travelled on the cars and never would, and the poor creature must have been marvelling in her dumb way why people should wander so far afield instead of staying where they were born. The little donkey's reflections were as plainly written on his countenance as if they had been uttered in pure Castilian as he stood a moment, an expressive silhouette, staring in bewilderment. "Demonios! what's that infernal machine about?" was his conclusion, whereupon he whirled around and scampered off, flinging his four legs in as many directions.

There was a change of trains at Manzanares, a settlement which in spite of its an-

A Street Vender.

On the Road to Argamasilla

tiquity and of its poetical name, looks a handful of houses scattered hap-hazard on the bare soil, like children's blocks in a nursery corner. However, it is alive and has one of the finest distilleries (bodegas) of Spain, where I caught a glimpse of the peasant workmen eating their lunch in a clean modern-built shed by a row of formidable jars, each of which, I was told, held some twelve hundred gallons of wine. To this day, as in the time of Cervantes, these jars of porous clay are exclusively manufactured in Toboso forever enshrined in the imagination of all lovers of romance as the home of Dulcinea, the one true love, ardent though platonic, of the last and most celebrated of knights errant. Brick-yards I saw and the many chalk mills, where gypsum is ground to powder for the manufacture of plaster of Paris, were old-fashioned and slovenly. In open paved areas, scattered everywhere in and about Manzanares, threshing was going on in the same primitive way as in the days of the Moors, the Romans, or the Iberians. A band of donkeys, horses, and mules were simply hitched to a flat board upon which the driver stood urging his team round and round in ever-narrowing circles till the pile of grain lay flat. But the half-naked, sunburned young drivers, balancing themselves on the narrow boards as if it were the easiest thing to do in the world, looked like living bronzes with their devil-may-care air and something of that same alertness, that poise and grace of movement one loves in the little Pompeian figures.

By the lonely station-building of Argamasilla, the one bit of life was the postal-carriage, a four-wheeled affair, springless, with insecure board benches under an arch of plaited straw covered with canvas. It was the hottest part of the day, and the hottest day of the year, the driver said, but it did not persuade him to spare his team. At the incessant cracking of his whip the four horses raced forward in a stampede, raising thick clouds of stinging dust which blurred completely road and landscape and produced the sensation of travelling in a furnace at white heat. The coach-dog barked, the board-seats rattled, while the vehicle creaked and plunged. Here was old-time travelling with a vengeance.

That part of me which is monopolized by

On the Road to Argamasilla

the artist—I shall call it my Quixote self—rather revelled in this excess of local color, but my Sancho Panza side, caked with dirt, shaken and bruised by the jolting, was in a deplorable condition. And yet could Sancho do aught but endure what could not be helped? His resigned martyrdom lasted for an hour, till a stop was made to water the horses. Thereafter, our pace relaxing, occasional glimpses could be had on either side of the road of fields of scorched wheat with each separate stem a shining, bristling spear. Before us the village of Argamasilla, "birthplace of Don Quixote," the guide-book says unblushingly, revealed more and more distinctly its white houses nestled under the

On the Road to Argamasilla

trees. The purple Sierras, dreamy sentinels of the plains, stood on the extreme border of the horizon. Above it all wonderfully shaped clouds made against the azure background an exquisite mosaic of translucent tones.

II

Argamasilla

The Amo.

Argamasilla

WE entered the pueblo with cracking whip. Not a soul was to be seen until the solitary, slouchy figure of the inn-keeper emerged from under the mat covering the door of the posada—*Al Parador del Carmen, Casa Gregorio*. Gregorio, hardly able to express his astonishment at the unusual sight of a guest, looked at the horses and said nothing. But the driver kindly ventured an introduction, "He is for you, Gregorio." "Yes," I added, "and for some time, I hope, Don Gregorio, if I may have a bed in your house." A "don" well placed never fails to please a Spaniard, even if he be that most independent and despotic of beings—

an inn-keeper of low order. "Of course, Señor, and why not?" and upon these slight preliminaries I followed Gregorio under the straw curtain.

My first look at the Parador del Carmen did my Quixote self good, for it was the most picturesque place imaginable. Here at last I had plunged from civilization and nineteenth century to the condition of ancient days, and apparently reached bottom. "Apparently," is said advisedly, for later on I was to see infinitely more primitive scenes. However, this first sensation at passing from the outside glare to that smelly, purplish interior, comfortless but plentiful of queer, dirty features, was intense.

After the manner of its ancestor, the Moorish caravanserai, this posada, like all others, was composed of a series of irregular constructions built around a courtyard. In the room in which I found myself the life of the place centred. Walls and pillars rose in confusion and arches opened unexpected vistas into dirty, odorous emptiness, streaked by stray blades of sunlight. Overhead close rows of blackened tree-trunks, forming the ceiling, were concealed under cobweb gar-

Muleteers in the Posada.

Argamasilla

lands, and hundreds of flies droned a ceaseless, loud murmur like the strings of a symphony, broken in upon by recurrent snores from limp bodies coiled in corners on the bare earth and by the sharp, insistent munching of the mules at their forage in the stables.

Following Gregorio upstairs I hastily arranged for the exclusive use of a little whitewashed room, fitted with three beds with bulky mattresses rolled on the boards—for here springs are unknown, of course—at the exorbitant price of ten cents a day—it was policy to propitiate this man Gregorio, the *amo*, the soul of this establishment — and then hurried down again to enchantment!

Argamasilla

But my Panza, rising in his might, insisted on something more substantial than sensations which he thought were not to be indulged in on an empty stomach. Unfeelingly I had to disturb the *amo*, who, seated on a stone bench, his head between his hands and his elbows on his knees, was evidently

wondering what manner of man was this stranger, dressed as a countryman, but with a queer stamp which he was unable to locate. Panza felt elated at the answer that it might be possible to have something to eat. "What can I have then, *amo?*" I continued. "*De todo* (Of everything), Señor," elusive abbreviation for "of all that you bring," and I had brought nothing. The fates were kind, however, for with the help of three females, a boy, and an old dilapidated character, a sort of buffoon, the *cojo*, necessary functionary of all posadas, whose duties are to run errands, amuse the household and be the butt of its jokes, a complicated tortilla was slowly manufactured. In a little dark room, the key of whose carefully locked door dangled at his belt, the *amo* went to fetch the ingredients which composed it — eggs, potatoes, onions, herbs, and ham, besides I know not what. When it was finally served on a bench and famished Panza seated before it, every one came slouching by. Was it that the strong odor

Argamasilla

of crude olive-oil was too attractive to be resisted or that the unusual spectacle of a man eating with fork as well as with knife could not be missed? Whatever it may have been, they, not unlike a pack of small dogs watching another dog munch his bone, sat or stood around observing each disappearing morsel till the oppression of these glittering eyes steadfastly fixed on my movements made me feel that something was expected and must  be done. I had not failed to offer a share of my tortilla to one and all before touching it, and now the psychological moment had come which must transform the silent watchers into friends, or else life would be a failure for the next few days. With my best manner I offered a draught of my wine around. It was refused, a customary denial, that, though going against the grain, is nevertheless religiously practised by high and low. A sec-

Argamasilla

ond and more familiar offer, "*Vamos, vamos hombres*" ("Come on, men"), brought each one to the mark. Then as the pig-skin bottle passed from hand to hand the place became alive. Cigarettes were lit, remarks ventured, questions asked and answered, and the song of the flies became but a distant accompaniment to human voices as the world of Argamasilla began unfolding itself before me.

Very like our world it was, yet characteristic in a hundred little and big ways. The manner of those half Moors, who like the natives of southern Italy are born for finessing, and love to reach their ends by slow, roundabout approaches, was fine to watch. After learning what they already knew, that I was a stranger (a term which applies to any one not a Manchegan) they dangled a variety of bait that should tempt me to disclose what manner of man I was and what I had come for. One imagines that if cats could, they would talk in just the way these people did—slowly, with the same imperturbable glare in their fixed, brilliant eyes. Figuratively speaking, these muleteers and inn folk ventured cautiously one paw here, one there, retreated, advanced, till enough facts having been secured, the pretty game ended. Then having learned what I wished to do, every-

one fell to giving me the benefit of his ideas and experiences. The most interesting were those of the chief courtier of the *amo;* a worthless, lazy chap, marked out by a greasy old cap sporting the fatidical initials of the bull ring, P. D. T. (*plaza de toros*), which

Argamasilla

proclaimed the wearer a lover and connoisseur of the great game.

"Yes, Señor, Don Quixote was a funny chap. It's a great book though and known to the whole world, even to the heathen and to the English and the others. I read it and found it droll reading, but the best of it I did not get. There is much in it for persons of learning. They all say who know that the science of the world is there, and that when you understand it you can get as rich as you want. But I am ignorant and was only amused. Don Quixote was a very ridiculous fellow surely! Think of his taking those wenches at the venta for castle maidens! *Jesù*, what an ass he was!"

"And Sancho, you say? Well, he is like you and me, he wants to eat and sleep and get along with everybody in a nice way. But then I don't know the book. There is something in it I can't get hold of which makes priests and the like read it over and over. Don Federigo, a lawyer, who lives now in Madrid, says there is not another book like it, so full of politics and everything."

"Sí, Señor, Argamasilla is full of Quixote. There is his portrait in the church, and his

One of the Rare Good Times of the Women.

house was torn down only a short time ago, and here is the gentleman (a general bow of the company to the citified-looking young man who then entered the place) who has installed a fine bodega on its site, as perfect a bodega as you have seen in Madrid. And we'll show you also the prison where Cervantes wrote the book."

A moderate distribution of wine brought a score of idlers and notables, who kept up the discussion on Quixote. And in such

Argamasilla

pleasant manner the rest of the day was passed. Late in the evening I sat with the *amo* in the darkness outside the door, under the sombre, lapis-lazuli sky clustered with stars. A trembling murmur, like the heaving of a calm sea, intensified all accidental noises, the barking of dogs, the jingling of the bells of the mules hurrying to their night's shelter. A laborer coming home from the fields passed at a gait, which one felt to be rapid, though the sound of his footsteps was deadened in the dust. He sang with a rich, full, uncultivated voice, a song of Andalusia, one of those *Malagueñas* which are replacing the distinctive provincial songs all over the peninsula. Each verse was a complete musical phrase, given as a trill and ending in a long-sustained guttural minor note, and there were long pauses between the verses.

> Nor with thee, nor without thee,
>   Have my troubles any remedy;
> With thee, because thou killest me,
>   And without thee, because I die of it.

The voice, alternately crying and sighing, kept its male ring, while the pathetic words

The Posada at Grape-Harvest Time.

Argamasilla

were flung into space with the most passionate expression. It was like the nightingale's song, as impulsive, as harmonious with the scene and hour, and long after the voice had died out in the distance my nerves kept vibrating to the inexpressibly wild melody as if the very silence was still full of the echoes of this riot of feeling.

Turning in at about ten the son of the *amo*, eighteen years old, is stretching himself on the floor over which he has spread his mantle. Under his head by way of pillow is the harness of his mules. "Why doesn't he sleep in a bed?" I inquire. "It's no use," says the *amo*. "At midnight he'll have to go to the fields and work. You see this is harvest-time and we must work day and night." I found out that "we" meant everyone else in the household but my host.

The following days gave me a good opportunity to see truly typical posada life. The *amo*, one of the rare, well-to-do persons of Argamasilla, owning vineyards and wheatfields, had to devote his early mornings and late afternoons to overseeing his laborers. He would come back usually at nine in the morning, with his son and some of his men,

Argamasilla

who had been up and at work at the threshing-ground since as early as three o'clock. All had then their first meal in common. The long knives were unsheathed; each man proceeded to cut a thin slice of bread, stuck the point of his knife into it and used it as a spoon to dip into the dish of hard peas and cucumbers, swimming in mixed oil and water, which was placed on a stool in the middle of the group. A new spoon had to be cut for each spoonful and much dexterity was needed, even with the help of one's thumb, to secure enough peas on the flat piece of bread. The *amo* passed the wine-bottle round but once, the men indulging in it sparingly. When a man had finished, he would wipe his lips with the back of the hand, get up and go to a stand where the water-pitcher was held, lift it and, holding it at arm's length, take a long draught, then lighting his cigarette, he would be off to work again. What a frugal diet! No wonder these peasants are such healthy creatures, solid and limber, that they walk with an elastic, light step and in repose seem ever ready to move, suddenly, without effort—the whole body ready to spring. Our

Argamasilla

notions of Spanish indolence are true enough of the "classes," but the peasants are as hard-working a people as can be found anywhere, performing their work on fare which not even the poorest Italians would find sufficient.

During the warm hours the *amo* remained

at home. A couple of parasites kept him company, smiled at his jokes and feasted on his sententious wisdom. While I was staying there Gregorio made himself a pair of shoes and his friends, enjoying the rare opportunity, sat and watched admiringly the

Argamasilla

progress of the work, occasionally indulging in a bit of dialogue, but the sturdiness, the sombre side of the national character would reveal itself in protracted periods of silence and repose when the cigarettes alone were alive. The fact that Gregorio was doing something became known in the neighborhood, and other idlers would come and join the circle from time to time and marvel how the worthy man did his work so well. Occasionally one of the group would get up,

wiping his forehead, to have a drink of water from the bottle, with some kindly meant word to the foreigner—"God, it's hot, Señor!" Flies were thick, dogs asleep, a girl was sewing in a corner while her favorite cat sat on a stool watching her. A strapping laborer would walk in with a nod and abbreviated "How do" toward the group and disappear in the stable. Were it not for these happenings the posada would have been as quiet as the town.

Upon this dull background of the posada life there defiled morning and night all sorts of types of muleteers—fantastic, wild-looking fellows, who strode in and out silently with hardly a glance at anyone. After taking care of their mules they would sit in a corner and eat the hard bread and bit of cheese they had brought with them, or lie down to sleep anywhere on the bare soil, with no covering over them and but a convenient stone for a pillow.

The women-folk, mother and two daughters, were left strictly alone. The *ama* had charge of the cooking, the ingredients for which were given to her by her husband after a good deal of noisy bickering, he claim-

Argamasilla

DON RODRIGO DE PACHECO.
From the painting in the Church of Argamasilla.

ing that she did not make the best of what he gave, she that he never gave her enough. The daughters, modest girls of pleasing looks, were working all the time, helping in the kitchen, keeping the three guest-rooms in order (when said rooms were occupied, which was not often), fetching water from the well, sprinkling the premises, or sewing. 'Twas

Argamasilla

all work and no play with them unless, once in a while, they indulged in quiet games with cats and puppies when the watchful eye of the *amo* was not on them. It was impossible not to sympathize with the *ama*, poor old woman, shrivelled and dried up by her slave life out of which no escape was possible without extreme mental, social, as well, alas! as physical troubles, more than she could bear. But out of those sunless days of harassing experiences she had unconsciously, perhaps, reached the highest point that kindly as against egotistical and brutish feelings can reach, fighting inch by inch the battle of a good woman against all that selfishness and arrogance embodies. She knew the purely temporary advantages she could get, that she could go no farther, and that it would be easier to condone and suffer silently. But she kept on undaunted, stubbornly true to her superior instinct, preaching by example and by words what was right and good. How she compelled my admiration and my respect! To watch for a time such situations, powerless to help in the slightest way, is one of the saddest experiences of the passing traveller.

His Favorite Chair in the Barber Shop.

The *amo's* return at sunset was the signal for supper, the making of which had its distinct local flavor. The kitchen was a large room, bare like the other rooms of the place but for an old chest, a table, and the hearth— a square of low brick flooring in a corner. Upon this hearth dried-up branches were set on fire, filling the room and transforming the cook and her assistants into witches in the midst of some infernal incantation. Gregorio's was a well-to-do family, having meat once a day during the harvest - time. In ordinary times, of course, they had it but once a week. The meat was always served in a sort of soup. The girls, with flowered kerchiefs around

their necks, the men in shirt-sleeves with red turban-like rags on their heads, barefooted all, dipped their wooden spoons democratically in the same bowl. There was no attempt at conversation, only at times the sharp voice of the *amo* would tell some laborer to go

Argamasilla

slow, warning him that he was eating more than his portion. The hanger-on before mentioned would sit against a pillar, his old frame bent over his staff, and, keeping his keen, knowing eyes looking steadfastly away from the table, appear perfectly indifferent to what was going on. Dogs had more rights in this house than he had, poor chap. Toward the middle of the dinner the *ama* would ask him to join the circle, whereupon Gregorio, venting his displeasure, would make chilling remarks, such as, "the door of the posada was as wide open as the gates of the city," to which the gentlemanly fellow would answer, mildly, "Yes, Señor, and I hope many good things may come in through it besides dust."

Yet Gregorio was not as bad as he seemed. He was a variety of the *Nouveau riche* type, having risen from the humblest beginnings through an unforeseen inheritance, and prosperity had proved too much for him. In spite of his parvenu arrogance of the desire to make his family and dependents feel that they owed their existence to him, he was, I believe, rather a good sort at bottom. And, after all, in judging people so far removed

Argamasilla

from us by their traditions, education, environment, their dismal isolation and lack of opportunities, one would better pause before rendering a radical judgment.

Such was the routine of the days at the posada. I was told that once a month, on market-day, all was bustle and movement, and that a dance was sometimes indulged in;

but Sundays were days like the others, except that the men improved the chance of making coarse remarks about the women going to church. There was, at least to me, mighty little religion and a great deal of superstition among these Argamasilla folk. The going to church was the one diversion in the terribly monotonous, hard life of the women, but the men preferred to sit or stand around the square, or on a friendly doorstep and in the same breath indulge in sneers at the priests and the Church and at professions of loyalty to "Our Lady."

It is difficult to get at the real feelings of these people on religion. The contrast of their poverty and hard-working lives makes them distrust the ease and comparative plenty of the priests, and they refuse to give a cent to the Church unless in sickness or in old age, as a sort of investment for great returns in this or the next world. After a fashion of their own they have reverential if not spiritual notions, but they can't help seeing the difference between the actions of their priests and true religion.—"No, Señor—they are in the Church to make a fine living out of it, not to be its humble and devoted servants. They won't pray for us unless we pay them!"

The Procuradores, representatives of the

The Plaza of Argamasilla on Market Day.

people of Castile, had given utterance to similar feelings centuries ago:

"*Que no quieren los villanos ni el vino del Sacramento si viene de vuestras manos.*"

The villeins would refuse even the Sacramental wine if given through your hands.

Argamasilla

Argamasillans, their pueblo having no industry of any sort, subsist entirely on the neighboring country, each villager renting some wheat or wine fields from a few land-owners, an aristocratic family in particular which owns the largest part of the surrounding district. The best of the crop, not a percentage but a fixed amount, goes to the land-owner, who is thus insured against bad crops, the tenant besides paying all the taxes, which are heavy. On one side no risks are taken, and the lack of income of the bad years is carried over to be made up in the prosperous years; thus the tenant is in a perpetual condition of indebtedness to the landlord, an indebtedness which keeps rolling up with usurious rates of interest, the only rates upon which consent to continuation of the lease can be secured. Landed proprietor here, as in the Italy of fifty years ago (and in many districts of Southern Italy today), means usurer.

This iniquitous system is another proof, if any were needed, of the decadence of Spain, the country where the communes conquered their rights against lords and kings as early, if not earlier, than in any other country in

Europe — where the achievements of the *Vaqueros* of Asturia, the *Hermandinos* of Galicia, the *Communeros* of Castile, the *Agermanados* of Valencia, the *Fueristas* of Catalonia, Aragon, Navarre, and Biscaye are among the most glorious of the contests for individual rights and liberty in the history of human progress. The poor Manchegan of to-day is not so much unlike the villein of feudal times obliged to pay tribute to king and lord, to grind his wheat in the mill and bake his bread in the oven of his lord; to live in the castle's shadow with no right to work elsewhere. It is true that he can take wife or give his daughter in marriage without the consent of a master, and that he can make his will, though in his condition this is rather an empty privilege.

The chief glory of Argamasilla is the Casa de Medrano, a solid stone house, whose main portion stands probably in the same position, but for the decay of age, as when Cervantes was kept a prisoner in its cellar.* There is

---

* The half-ruined part of the house, connected by a single narrow doorway with the part now standing in good condition, shows plainly the Moorish influence on the social conditions of the time, for it was the prison-like harem where the women of the house were kept away from any possible intrusion.

Argamasilla

little doubt that this is the very place where the design of the book, which was "engendered in a prison" (see prologue to the first part of Don Quixote), was first moulded. Some twenty-five feet by eight, and seven feet high, with a mere hole for window, this unhealthy cell is so dark that when the original door, still partly standing, with its iron clamps and nails, is closed, it precludes the possibility of Cervantes having been able to write in it. But to say this would be to the Argamasillans a personal insult. Cervantes says that the book, as the "child of my wit," was conceived in a prison, which satisfies the Argamasillans that the whole book, even the second part, written ten years later than the first, was entirely written in this cellar!

The villages of New Castile fight fiercely

The Dance at the Posada.

Argamasilla

for the honor of having given birth to Cervantes or to his hero. There are local traditions used and invented to prove, by long foolish dissertations, too many of them in printed book form, that Cervantes and Quixote did all sorts of things in each of the villages. At a low computation, taking into account only the most persistent claimants, Cervantes was born in six different places. Yet he lived unappreciated and in misery. And his masterpiece, which has become the property of mankind, and of whose three hundred editions more than half are other than Spanish, was for more than a century and a half only a sort of chap-book for the million. In Spain, particularly, it was regarded as scarcely deserving of attention by men of letters. The recognition of its worth first came from England. " Spain may have begotten the child, but England was its foster-mother" (H. W. Watts). The Spaniards have since scrambled frantically to do tardy justice to the " Prince of the Spanish Geniuses." Thus a tribute has been paid in this very spot by one of its children. In this same Casa de Medrano, some thirty years ago, Rivadeneyra established a printing-office for the sole purpose of issuing two beautiful editions of Don Quixote, and an Infanta pulled from the press the first sheets of the large edition.

This house, with its precious historical associations, is now the abode of a village personage who alternates the functions of postmaster with his trade of cobbler. I sometimes gave him the pleasure of leaving his humble cobbler's bench to assume his important governmental functions — a transformation he enjoyed as much as I did. He would receive with great respect these missives for strange countries and remain pondering upon the fact that so many days were needed to speed them on to their destination, and that Americano postmen should handle these letters entrusted to his faithful hands. He would follow them on their way, and at each new meeting venture opinions as to how far they had gone, so that his gratification, when about leaving La Mancha I informed him of the safe arrival of my first letters, was great. "Thank God! Señor, our postal service is perfection!"

The extraordinary interest manifested in Cervantes now points to a national honor

Argamasilla

which each village tries to monopolize. In this country of contrasts, where the differences of climate and surroundings have made the peninsula a land of well-defined provinces, with distinct habits and costumes evolved from the conditions of each separate *milieu*, patriotism is sectional. "I am not a Spaniard, I am a Catalan," expresses the general attitude. But here, in La Mancha, villages

Argamasilla

are up in arms against other villages, simply on account of Cervantes. Beyond doubt, however, it is proved that Miguel de Cervantes was born in Alcalá de Henares, a town of New Castile, east of Madrid, and that in Argamasilla the "meagre, shrivelled, whimsical" child of his genius was conceived. There are also strong probabilities of truth in the local claim that the original of Quixote was Don Rodrigo de Pacheco, one of the hidalgos of Argamasilla at the time of Cervantes's appearance in the town as royal collector of taxes. It was by the authority of Rodrigo

Argamasilla

that Cervantes was imprisoned in the cellar of the Casa de Medrano, and Rodrigo's house, lately destroyed, corresponded in its main points with the description in the book. In an old painting, which is preserved in the parish church, he and his niece are kneeling before the Virgin thanking her for her assistance, as set forth in the quaint description at the bottom of the picture:

Our Lady appeared to Don Rodrigo de Pacheco on the eve of St. Matthew, in the year 1601, and cured him—who had promised her a lamp of silver, and called day and night upon her in his great affliction— of a great pain he had in his brain through a chilliness which had fallen into it.

The good priest, Cervantist by birth and choice, who had accompanied me to the church, and who was pleased at my interest in the picture, diplomatically disguising the object of his argument under flowers of Castilian rhetoric, tried to make me agree with him and the Argamasillans. I was not conscious that I failed to realize that there was Don Quixote in flesh and blood. The high

Argamasilla

cheek-bones and wandering eyes seemed Don Quixote enough, though the sensual full lower lip hardly so. But later on I became convinced that my enthusiasm was not freely enough displayed to reassure my new acquaintance, for he stuck to me during my stay in Argamasilla, going so far as to often abandon his favorite chair in the barber-shop to convince me again and again that Don Rodrigo was undoubtedly the original of Don Quixote. He had hopes that on my return home I should stand up boldly, challenging all-comers to disprove that important fact, and thereby exalt the fame and glory of his town in that far-away America, which, in spite of all past Spanish experiences, remains in the popular mind a mysterious El Dorado with wonderful vegetation and full of gold. And Americans, in spite of their queer uncivilized manners and mode of life, are strangely attractive to these good peasant folk, who consider them all — for there is hardly any knowledge of a North and South, of an English and Spanish America— half-breed descendants of the great Conquistadores and the Indians—some sort of bastard children of Spain, who have grown rich

Argamasilla

at the expense of the mother country, and yet whose power redounds to the glory of the Spanish family!

My friend the priest went so far as to post his niece at an upper window of his comfortable house to watch should I happen to pass in the lonely street, so that he might know where I went, and go and button-hole me. The duty can hardly have been irksome to the damsel—it chimed in too well with local customs, for at the approach of footsteps in the usually deserted streets the latticed windows would always be seen to blos-

Argamasilla

som for an instant with inquisitive female faces. This curiosity is never offensive, and one can't help feeling thankful at being a source of innocent distraction to people whose life turns hopelessly in the same narrow circle. Wherever I went wiles were resorted to to look at me without impertinence. Some fortuitous duty had to be performed, the street had to be sprinkled, or the woman was apparently immersed in conversation on her neighbor's threshold, gesticulating about something which was not said, with eyes and ears fixed on that most unusual sight—an Americano in Argamasilla.

On the last evening before my first sally, Gregorio and I had a walk through the village, kicking the thick-lying dust and knocking our feet on the rough stones of the irregular streets without sidewalks. Here and there stood a stranded cart, groups sat silently before open doors—the lights, in that harmony of gray and purple, pitching in a warm note like a gaudy flower in the dark hair of an Andalusian girl. The customary salutations were exchanged in a low, grave voice — 'Go your way with God" accompanied us on our way. We sat on the little

Argamasilla

bridge which spans that curious river the Guadiana, and in the dense foliage over us the nightingales were singing, and little falls near by murmuring an accompaniment. Gregorio told many a story which had the musty perfume of bygone, forgotten days, about this wonderful Guadiana, that had its birth in swamps, and after running for miles loses itself, to reappear seven leagues farther on.  "Very mysterious, isn't it?" says my companion. "Once one of the kings of Spain was talking about his country with the king of France, and to his chagrin was finding that all that Spain had, France also had. It had olives and wheat and grapes, and everything that Spain had, until the king thought of the Guadiana, and he said: 'I have a bridge seven leagues in length.' The poor French king had nothing further to

Argamasilla

say." There, come down by way of mouth through generations, altered but clearly recognizable, was the story of the Ambassador Rui Gonzalez de Clavijo, sent by Enrique III. to Tamerlane, and who, having in mind this same Guadiana, boasted that in his master's dominions was a bridge forty miles wide, on the top of which two hundred thousand herd of cattle could graze.

III
The Cave of Montesinos

A Ruidera Street Scene.

The Cave of Montesinos

I WAS fortunate during my first week in Argamasilla in enlisting the services of Ezechiel, an honest old fellow, possessor of a mule cart, and fairly acquainted with the surrounding districts. For many days thereafter Ezechiel and I rambled over this poor land of La Mancha; and if I had to pay for my delightful experiences in some bodily discomforts, they were part of the game and were more than compensated for by constant intercourse with plain, old-time folks, by the superb scenery, with its ruined castles and caravansaries, relics of feudal and Moorish days, by the ancient customs and the legends which, like ivy on a gnarled oak-tree, cling to every bit of this historical and romantic land.

It is a little before two in the morning when, for the first time, I find Ezechiel at the posada door loading provisions, hard-boiled eggs, loaves of bread, skin bottles of wine and water, and the inseparable compan-

The Cave of Montesinos

ion of every Manchegan, the shot-gun, in his two-wheeled cart. A few steps, and like Panza and Quixote "we sally forth from the village without any person seeing us," and are in the wide, flat country. In spite of the darkness, a sort of translucence permeates sky and earth, giving to the scene the weird aspect of a country of dreams. The faint, shadowy silhouettes of the escort of two mounted police, "Guardias Civiles," bob up and down before us like intangible images. Our mule vanishes in the gloom; the only things truly alive are two stars—two watching eyes peeping above the horizon. Stretched on one of the two benches which

The Cave of Montesinos

line the cart, I doze peacefully, lulled by the subdued breathing of old mother earth in her sleep—the grand lullaby made by all the infinitesimal noises of nature, above which the fitful jingling of the bells played a delightful silvery cadence.

Steadfastly, up and down invisible hills, the cart advances on its monotonous journey into the solitude, creaking like a creature in pain. Once in awhile, like a warrior preparing for the assault, our mule stops an instant, gathering strength to bump against and surmount some inevitable obstacle, and then follows a bounce on the rude benches and occasionally a landing on the rope

The Cave of Montesinos

netting which forms the bottom of the cart.

As day approaches, the country reveals itself in a series of slowly changing panoramas. The dreary plain is left behind, and the sav-

age and picturesque scenery of the *Monte* now surrounds us. How naturally the two pathetic figures of Quixote and Sancho loom up in this admirable setting, and harmonize with the grandiose, severe lines of the rocky hills surmounted by ruins. We pass by scores of *batañes* (fulling-mills), which Cervantes may have had in mind in his advent-

The Cave of Montesinos

ure of the Fulling-Hammers (Chapter XX.), for the surroundings of rocks and tall trees chime well with his description. The peasants who manned them in Cervantes's time must have been in appearance, type of face and costume, very like the brawny Arab-looking fellows we meet, and the range of ideas and style of living of these cannot be essentially different from that of their ancestors. The mills themselves, bearing signs of extreme old age, make pretty pictures, with their dripping moss and maiden-hair garments. It would be agreeable to think they are the same *batañes* which gave such tremendous sensations to the worthy Knight and frightened his faithful Squire, but the impossible adventures of the hero of romance have been made to agree with the stern facts of geography, and in consequence we know, as Cervantes probably did not, that the *batañes* he described were located in a definite place east of Ciudad Real.

The roadway begins to skirt the lagoons of Ruidera, the chain of lapis lazuli mirrors set in crowns of luxuriant rushes, formed by the Guadiana, the mighty river of Don Quixote's country. Toward nine, while catching

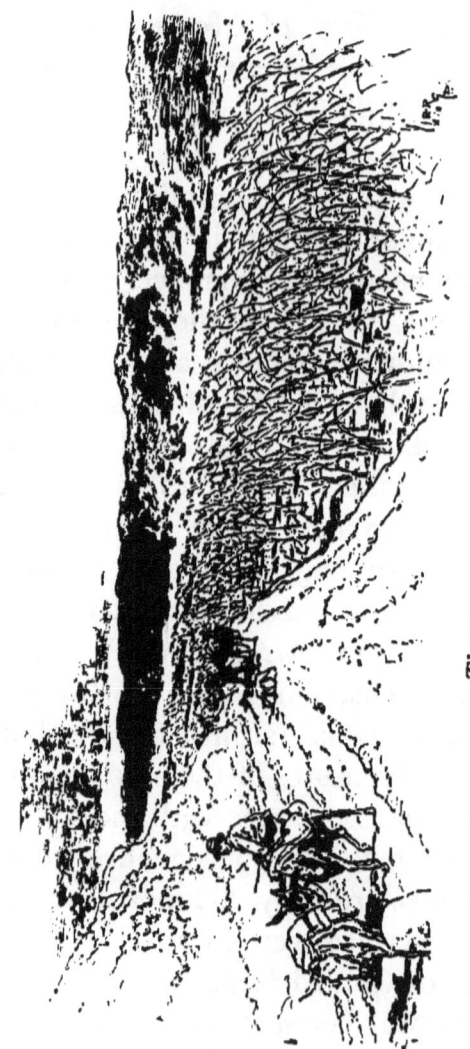

The Lagoons of Ruidera.

The Cave of Montesinos

a glimpse of a waterfall, we stumble on Ruidera, a handful of straggling houses singularly dwarfed by the huge ruins of a palace once one of the lordly seats of the mighty Order of San Juan, whom Cervantes served in the lonely capacity of tax collector. As we enter the one street ("street" by courtesy and for want of a fit name to describe it) I suddenly realize why Argamasillans have reason to be proud of their village. Argamasilla is a modern, civilized city compared to these tumble-down houses, with doors broken or hanging by ropes or propped up by stones, or gates without doors, and the shocking display of filth and decay everywhere.

The cart is left to sizzle in the sun. Our Guardias hold court, surrounded by effusive villagers, while I seek refuge from the heat in the house which gives shelter to travellers. A woman-servant, young, faded, and wrinkled, her clothes bundled about her hips, her hair a-tangle, sets out to brush away the inches of venerable dust which cover the beaten earth flooring. She moves about with the queer, nervous movements of a mountain goat, and, when I order her to desist, jumps

The Cave of Montesinos

as if struck and gives a wild, frightened look around. Ezechiel has a hard time to entice her to the courtyard and open-air cooking. The whitewashed walls of the show-room, the one room of this hostelry of the lowest order, the ceiling of smoked logs, the jugs and dried-skin bottles in the corner, the harness hung on a nail, vie with each other in hiding their identity under alternate coats of dirt, soot, and dust. Two impossible sofas parade as ornaments more than as useful objects, their flat cushions and pillows, filled with rags, keeping faithfully the impressions of the last impact. There are no windows, but a cool blue light falls from the chimney-shaft, and blades of sunlight coming through the holes and cracks of the closed door streak

The Cave of Montesinos

the shadow, making the millions of whirling atoms glisten.

While preparations for the dinner are going on outside, the Guardias drop in and regale me with as pretty a scene from the Spanish picaresque novels as one could wish for. They are, of course, above tips of any kind and are strictly enjoined to partake but of their own fare, which they carry with them everywhere in their journeys. But here what a godsend is the rare traveller able to command—meat for his dinner and probably, also, wine in profusion. And how can one help being near the traveller when meal-time

The Cave of Montesinos

approaches to make one's self agreeable, saying all sorts of nice things with a smile which unconsciously discovers the rows of short, sharp, white teeth ready for the fray! Honest Ezechiel had warned me against the snares sometimes set on such occasions, yet I couldn't but take pleasure in giving in at once (a great mistake), telling them that, of course, I hoped they would accept their share of my meal. The prey proving so easy, straightway the scope of my new friends' and parasites' operations grew to large proportions. Why shouldn't they rearrange the details of my trip so as to give themselves as little travelling and as many feasts as pos-

The Cave of Montesinos

sible? The most captivating reasons, enlivened with Castilian pearls of rhetoric and flowery and courteous expressions, flowed as naturally from their lips as water from a spring. I enjoyed it for a half hour, till it became clear that the stranger, who was falling from the dignity of Excellencia to that of Caballero, and finally of plain Señor, had reasons, and good ones, though my friends couldn't understand them, for keeping to his original plan. Nevertheless they kindly stood on each side of me during my repast, and valiantly helped fight the swarms of flies which threatened each morsel. I expected my huge skin wine-bottle to be in a state of collapse at the end of their dinner, but was hardly prepared for the Guardias's hasty departure and return with an enormous pan of wine-punch some villagers had prepared for them, a performance which was repeated several times. The Guardia Civil, this flower of special Spanish growth, half-military and half-police, which has worked by its *esprit de corps* so great a change in the brigand-ridden provinces of Spain, and has justly deserved the honored title of terror of evil-doers, is apt at times, when in the back country

The Cave of Montesinos

where communications are difficult and the ignorance and fear of the peasants insure immunity, to relax somewhat from its high estate and indulge in such undignified performance as this. Yet the failings of a few do not impair the great value and high character of a body of some twenty-eight thousand men, which, taken in its *ensemble*, is admirably disciplined and renders the most valuable services.

When I got ready to start off again toward noon my worthy protectors were lying limp in all their imposing military paraphernalia on the sofas above described, snoring like angry bulls, and I was grateful at being able to go without them.

As we march away from the river we find the country savage and desolate. Red earth-mounds surround us for hours with peculiar clusters of low, stunted trees, looking like flocks of sheep. The thermometer marks 100 degrees in the shade, yet the furnace air is dry, full of ozone, and rich with the pungent aroma of wild mountain plants. In a delicious monotony of surroundings the hours pass, enlivened only by the songs of the whirring, bustling, leaping locusts. How

In Ruidera.

The Cave of Montesinos

true is the Spanish equivalent for our "dog-days"—*canta la chicharra*—the song of the locusts and cicadas rejoicing in the heat, which serves but to make the silence of the solitude heard. In the good places the springless, unwieldy cart, with its solid iron axle, moves in a constant tremor, enlivened by occasional bumps. In bad places the process is reversed, and occasional rumbling lulls are the momentary diversions to the continual rough, bumping dance. Our wiry little mule bravely marches on at an even pace, and picking her way daintily among the loose stones carries her load over the rough road as if it were mere play. She is a good representative of her class, while her master

The Cave of Montesinos

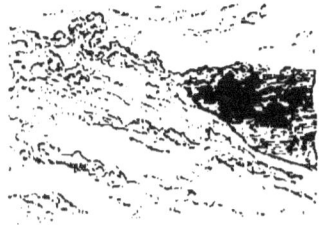
is a rare specimen of the muleteer fraternity. He has not even a whip, but his mule understands well the meaning of his words. Up the steep hill, he keeps up a constant stream of interjections to encourage her—" *Hija!* " "*Morena!*" " Daughter!" " Brunette!" "One more, daughter!" "Good!" "Go ahead!" " Beauty!" "*Aya!*" "*Arrarha!*" —"There we are," the brave brute making a visible effort at each word. When the top is reached Ezechiel rewards her with "*Guapa*," " Beauty," "Take it gently now, beauty," and with his quiet voice falls into praising the mule, which is his fortune. He could verily say of her what Sancho said of his ass: "O child of my bowels, born in

The Cave of Montesinos

my very home, the delight of my wife, the envy of my neighbors, the sharer of my burdens, and, beyond all, the support of half my person; for, with six and twenty maravedis, which thou earnest for me daily, do I make half my living." Ezechiel has a wife, and if he does not name her (for that would be contrary to custom), one feels that she occupies the whole background of his thoughts. I learn that they are very much concerned now, for the pig they are fattening does not come on well. Like all Manchegos, he rents a little field from some rich land-owner, which supplies potatoes and wheat to pay the land-owner, and enough besides, when all goes well, to keep the wolf from the door.

The Cave of Montesinos

To get an idea of the smallness of Ezechiel's income one has but to know that the only money which comes into the family is earned by his occasional journeys with his cart, doing errands and hauling freight. He has an average of a month out of the year at such work, and about four pesetas a day (at the time of my journey less than sixty cents in gold), out of which he must pay for the shelter and sustenance of himself and his mule during these trips. What little money is made goes toward paying for the rent of the house, buying the few household and farming implements and the cotton and wool out of which the wife makes their clothes.

The Cave of Montesinos

Late in the afternoon, having met with no one since leaving Ruidera, we pass through Osa de Monteil, the houses half-hidden in clouds of dust raised by the threshing going on all about. An hour after, Ezechiel,

who has never been in this direction before, loses his bearings, and we have a painful trudge across the brush till the yawn-

The Cave of Montesinos

ing chasm of the valley of the Guadiana is again before us. It is not easy to locate the object of our journey, the famous Cave of Montesinos, "of which so many and such wonderful things are" still "told in these parts," and we are about to give up the quest when a goatherd comes to our rescue. It was fitting that such a quaint figure as that of the lonely shepherd we met, dressed in the primitive costume which has not changed for centuries, with the crooked staff in hand and a horn dangling by his side, should be our guide to the mysterious place. On examination it is evident that Cervantes knew it, for his artistic description, cunningly exaggerated to suit the necessities of the romance, is true to nature and full of local

The Cave of Montesinos

color. The "Vagabond in Spain" was mistaken in placing the recess or chamber of which Quixote speaks as on the left hand of the cave going down. It is on the right hand, as in the story. The fact is not without value, since the "Vagabond" infers from it that Cervantes had not seen, but only heard of, the cave. Not being equipped with the needful lights, I could not fathom the mysterious recesses of the cave, which did not surprise Ezechiel or the shepherd, who were sure that no living man ever could go far into it, as there were insurmountable obstacles in the way—treacherous ground, a fathomless lake, a turbulent stream, and Heaven knows what! "Surely there are lots of gold and diamonds there," they said; and thus involuntarily testified to the persistence of traditions, for it is more than probable that the Cave of Montesinos is but an old Roman copper-mine. The weirdness of its surroundings is unimaginable.

The mixture of severity and loveliness makes of these valleys of the Upper Guadiana one of the rarest, most intimate, and impressive successions of landscapes I have ever seen. In the early evening, when the

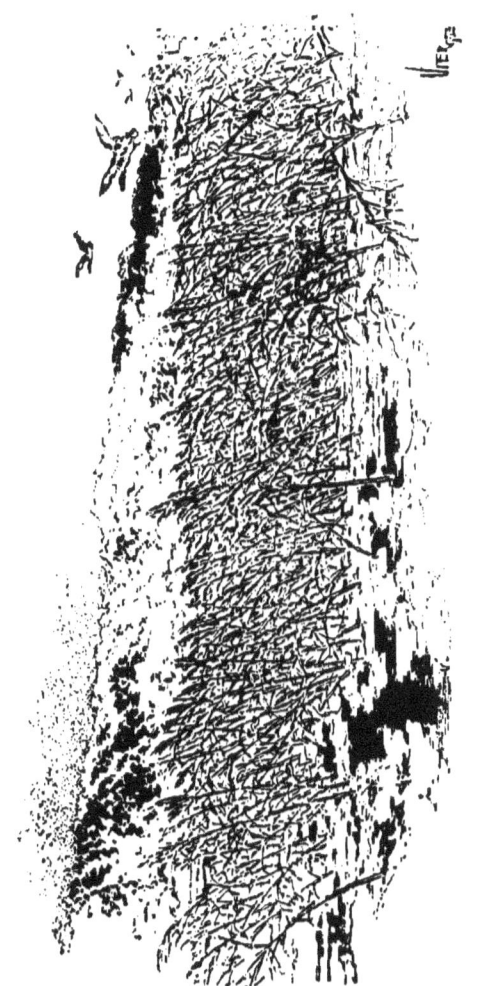

The Edge of a Lagoon.

The Cave of Montesinos

tender, delicate blush of the sky after sunset is streaked with veils of light, the earth has a solidity of aspect and a soberness and strength of color which the sunlight takes away from it.

IV

Monteil

The Hermitage of Saelices.

Monteil

IT is dark night when after leaving the cave of Montesinos we arrive at the Cortijo de St. Pedro, or at the three houses baptized with that florid appellation. We have had our supper on the road and I am too tired to watch the new mood of our friends, the Guardias, who be it said to their credit look somewhat ashamed of themselves. Getting into the hovel, some ten by fifteen feet in size, which is to be my night's lodging-place, I find the luxury of clean sheets over a straw mattress on one of the two stone benches on each side of the fire-place; on the other bench a youth stretched at full length and sleeping peacefully. The Guardias all dressed but for their boots, which they take off, lie down to sleep on the floor, and, thanks to habit and the glories of the *déjeuner*, succeed. Besides the entrance-door there are two doorless passages, one leading to the closet monopolized by the *amo* and his wife, the other to the stable. Sleep is impossible; the very stone under my mattress teems with animal activity, but I prefer lying awake to going outside where the cold mist of the neighboring marshes is saturated with malaria. Toward one in the morning some muleteer loudly knocks for admittance. The *amo* gets up, lights his oil-lamp (that of the Romans of old and the Moors of to-day), and in scampers a troop of mules to the stable; but as there is no place there for all, the new-comer stretches on the floor of our room between two of his mules, whose nervously tinkling bells tell tales of martyrdom, as do also the plaintive sounds, the groans, and quick motions of the restless sleepers.

Oh! dura tellus Iberiæ!

At last, unable to stand any more, I leave the room and urge Ezechiel to start while I make an excursion to the Ermita de Saelices, the same Hermitage mayhap, *quien sabe?* where Don Quixote, Sancho, and the student stopped on their way back from the Enchanted Cave of Montesinos, and where, not having·the good fortune of finding the Hermit at home, but only his she deputy (a by no means uncommon appanage of hermitages in those days), they were unable to

Monteil

secure what Sancho so much wanted there—a draught of good wine. "If it had been a water thirst, there are wells on the road where I could have quenched it," was the squire's blunt acknowledgment for the woman's offer of the tame substitute. At small expense the chapel could be restored to its original condition, so well built it is. But hermits are no more the fashion of the day, and the numerous army of priests and monks has been so reduced that all over the land, which is yearly growing poorer, most of the churches and chapels are falling to ruins.

A man whom we find prowling about the house offers a helping hand to harness the mule. As

we move away Ezechiel says: "You saw that man; he is to go to prison soon. He has killed his brother, the poor fellow." The case is typical of the temper of these people. This man Carlos had a brother Miguel, who one morning lately amused himself by throwing stones at Carlos's dog. Carlos, hearing his dog yell, came out, saw what Miguel was doing and told him to stop. Miguel refused to do so, adding that if his brother did not go back to the house and stop talking he would throw stones at him too. Whereupon Carlos went back to the house, got his gun, and coming back to the

Monteil

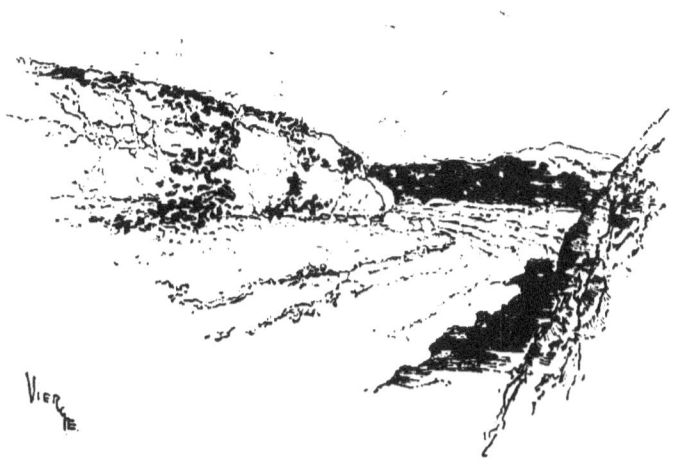

door-step, shot his brother and killed him. I asked Ezechiel, "What made Miguel torment the dog? Had he been bitten by him?" Ezechiel says: "No; I think not; but you see Miguel had a large family of daughters. You know the saying: '*Tres hijas y una madre, cuatro diablos para un padre.* Three daughters and a mother, four devils for a father.'" "Why is Carlos free?" I asked. He replied: "Well, they'll take him to prison when his trial comes on in a month or so." "Aren't they afraid he will run away in the meantime?" "No; where do you want him to run to, Señor? He can't hide in the

Sierras, for the Guardias will find him easily. He can't take a train and go anywhere, for he has never been on the cars in his life any more than I have, and he wouldn't know where to go."

I inquired what the penalty for such an offence was likely to be.

The old man replied: "I don't know; perhaps ten years, but probably less. You see there was provocation!"

We skirt the banks of the lagoons, and a succession of exquisite little Corot pictures follow one another at each new turn of the road. A gray gauze envelops them, blotting out the details and leaving only impres-

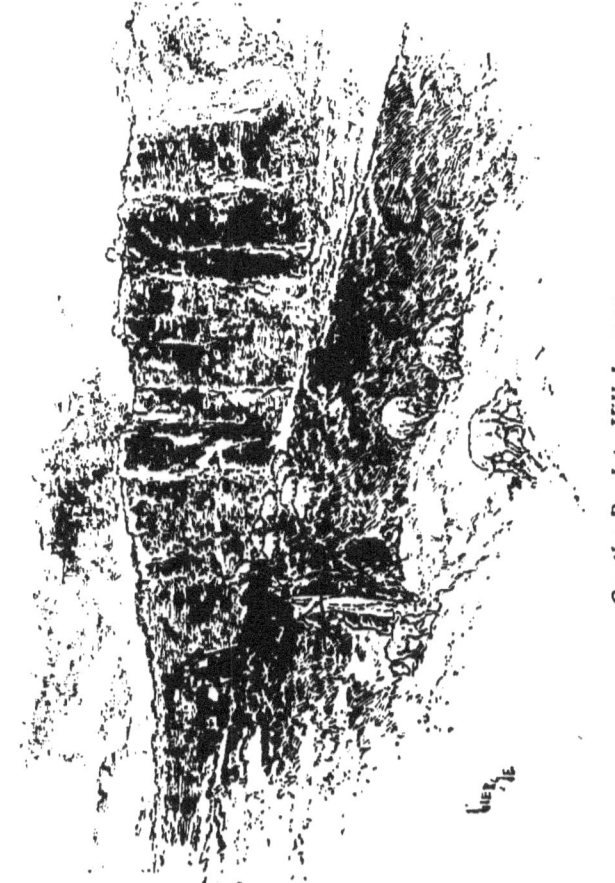

On the Road to Villahermosa.

sions of large masses in quiet tones under the opaline sky. Passing by the Castle of Rochafrida, its hoary, rambling walls, some fifteen feet thick, pierced by a few small openings, its huge crenellated towers crowning still the rocky inlet which rises solitary from the sea of reeds in the centre of a lake, look so terribly solid and massive as to bring forcibly to one's imagination the mediæval days. The site has a character of grandeur ; the hills on both sides of the lake showing their bare flanks, streaked with strange metallic colors, reds, yellows, and purples, in bands and in masses, alternating in ruthless barbaric splendor, emphasized by the few gnarled, dwarfed trees growing crookedly in the crevices. The contrast of all that savage barrenness with the beautiful lake and the rows of centenarian chestnuts on its shores with their noble masses of foliage is fine. But above it all, how this castle, "like roosting falcon musing on the chase," focuses the attention ! What a strange thing it is to nineteenth century eyes, and how forcibly it typifies that period of the development of humanity during which our race stumbled along in the traces

Monteil

of the feudal régime. The Carlovingian legends, full of simple humanity, which are entwined about these ancient stones come up to one's memory as not so distant after all. And the damsel Rosaflorida's love and courtship of brave Montesinos is quite new-womanlike.

We cross the marshes at the end of the Rochafrida lagoon, climb slowly up the hill, and find ourselves over the ridge on a deserted plain, broken in low undulations—an immense sea of reddish clay dotted with a few low junipers and briars. Our road is like those caravan roads of Africa—hundreds of yards in width, and made of a multitude of paths crossing one another, mixing together pell-mell, among which the mule picks the easiest with unerring instinct. That road is for hours the solitary evidence of human passage in the whole landscape, until at length, in a suddenly abrupt depression, the cañon bed of a winter torrent, we spy some shepherds with their flocks of sheep. Going out of our way we hail them, wanting to talk with them. They nod their heads and move sullenly away, and it seemed to me as if, being what they were, that was the most

Monteil

natural thing for them to do. One does not spend all one's life in such places without being affected by their forlornness and desolation. It is arid, savage La Mancha which makes the Manchegan peasants shy, taciturn, and sombre. These traits, always more or less prominent in all Spaniards, are they not largely due to the same cause—the lonely and savage character of the country?

Toward ten, at the end of a weary, tortuous climb, we come to some houses clustered around a big, ugly church. If ever the name of a town has belied its appearance it is the name of this sordid village, Villahermosa! It is needless to describe its hovel of a posada, or the miserable lunch which we found

Monteil

in it. Suffice it to say that as soon as our mule could be made ready we were off again for a reconnoissance some miles south toward Monteil, in chase of romantic compensations for the trivial hardships of my Sancho self.

And I found them straightway in the rough descent to the valley, where the mule stumbling, our cart turned a somersault. We had an amusing time making repairs, and were quite ready to start again when a

comely young woman stopped to exchange views of the affair with Ezechiel. She was mounted on a donkey, had her baby and some bundles in her arms and managed to hold a couple of loaded mules, besides gesticulating freely. After some good-natured chaff the little group scampered down the steep incline at a lively trot, and we followed more cautiously. Two leagues away, across the plain, were scattered, like huge monsters asleep, some queerly shaped mounds, on the highest of which was what remained of the famous Castle of Monteil. What a revelation of the old days these ruins were, and how they completed the pictures evoked by the Castle of Rochafrida! Each new impression of my rambles in La Mancha confirmed or helped the others, giving me the opportunity I sought of placing the adventures of the Knight of the Rueful Countenance in their original setting. At the foot of the castle, in the midst of the great mountain-fringed plateau, the eight or ten lesser rocky hills lie low like vassals of the forbidding old castle. Such a sight as this, typifying chivalry and the feudal idea, must have made Don Quixote happy. That im-

Monteil.

Monteil

pregnable fortress, whose walls will withstand the injuries of time as stoutly as the rock on which they are built, is like an eagle's aerie, the home from which the master, with his tenantry in the hovels of the village at his feet, dominated the whole tributary region around. From there he would start and prey upon vassals and neighbors. Times have changed for the better, even in Spain.

The little settlement—a typical mountain village—has an Alpine look, every little stone of its houses and pavements sticking out, bleak, colorless, gnawed by the hard teeth of the elements. Its tortuous streets are haunted by fine specimens of picturesque humanity, sane, clear-eyed, proud of bearing, and dressed like their ancestors of three centuries ago. At the door of the posada where we have a draught of the dry heady wine of Monteil, the conversation turns naturally on semi-historical, semi-legendary events, which are as real to these people, nay, more real than the contemporary happenings of Madrid or Cuba, and I am urged to visit the neighboring fields where the last battle of the war waged between Don Pedro, the Cruel, and

Monteil

Henry of Trastamara was fought, in March, 1369, and where Henry murdered his king and brother, unfairly held down by some French Knights, whose conscience rebelled at striking Don Pedro themselves, but permitted them to aid and abet the foul deed. Our audience worked itself up into a frenzy against the French Knights of 1369. "These pigs of foreigners, we would settle it with them, but they have never dared come back since," said the most rabid.

That such pages of history should remain vividly impressed on the minds of these nineteenth century ignorant folk, and still be so

Monteil.

Monteil

much a part of their life, seems wonderful to us who, concerned mainly with the things of the immediate present, cast but rare glances into the past. But when one realizes how familiar these peasants are with the old romances, it seems as if the moral of human development and civilization halted in places, for these Spaniards of to-day are very much like the English of the Elizabethan period, whose minds were filled with the legendary adventures of the heroes of precisely the same romances. Tusserand, in his "English Novel in the Time of Shakespeare," shows that translations and adaptations of the ancient Portuguese and Spanish books of chivalry, of which the "Amadis" is the type, were as popular in England as they had already become in France and in Germany. Later, even, Johnson on a visit to Bishop Perry found "Don Belianis," and sitting in the garden, devoured it to the end, and one of those interminable novels of chivalry was a great favorite of Burke. De Foe, in whose novels the reaction against the romantic tradition first asserted itself, was greatly influenced by the Spanish picaresque novels, especially the "Lazarillo," a great favorite also of Cervantes, which had been in Spain a satiric protest against romances and the assertion of the common people, of the every-day things of life.

Realism and Romanticism are no new terms—certainly not new things. The contemporary battle between the realistic novels and the tales of adventure was fought long ago in old Spain. But while in other western European countries the pendulum has since swung back and forth, Spain, living in the past, has to-day the same popular literature which England borrowed from her during the Elizabethan period. It was greatly relished then and endured long in

Villahermosa.

the guise of stories for children (Steele, in "The Tattler," speaking of his visits to his friend's son—the typical boy of the period, old enough to enjoy a good story—pictures him as greatly delighted with these old tales).

The coarsely printed little chap books, the single sheets adorned with rough woodcuts which pedlers sell or give as a premium to purchasers in the fairs of La Mancha, all tell the same old adventures of Christian chevaliers, castle damsels and Moors. Galdos, Valdés have not made the slightest headway in the popular imagination. They find their audience in the cities—the country is still devoted to the enchanted adventures of knights-errant which Cervantes warred against.

We pass silently over the scene of this fratricidal butchery—the Castle of Monteil looming up solitary behind, while before us Villahermosa stretches a purplish silhouette of houses, like a low battlement dominated by the massive tower of its church—under a tragic sky with a bloody squadron of fantastically shaped clouds scurrying along like an army in rout. The north wind blows a gale,

Monteil

and it is cold. July is the warmest month of the year in these parts, yet even in July, though it often is over a hundred in the shade during the hot hours of the day, heavy jackets and mantles are worn morning and evening. At the miserable posada we are glad of a place in the circle of silent guests squatted before the scanty fire of brushwood, while on our backs the wind blows from the doorless arched opening into the court-yard.

Our return journey to Argamasilla took some sixteen hours over a rarely used trail,

Sleeping Quarters at Villahermosa.

Monteil

cutting straight across country. The scenery of savagely bare plateaus, tawny and rocky and fragrant little wooded valleys, reminded me of the Corsican Mountains, probably because my companion had cautioned me to keep a sharp lookout and have my gun handy. Ezechiel's mongrel cur, he who was never to be seen and followed us in the shadow of the cart, must be added to my list of knowing brutes, for, as if conscious of his duty, he now kept patrolling the ground before and about us in a most thorough and business-like manner. There are no brigands in La Mancha, but any *arriero* whom one meets might feel tempted to shoot someone, and run the risk of getting a few cents or even nothing for his trouble.

We stopped to lunch by the side of a well, a favorite resort of flocks of wild pigeons who kept circling above our heads and showing by their sudden charges how they resented our intrusion. Farther on the temptation to hunt could hardly be resisted—all one had to do to bag one's supper was to stroll along the edge of the woods while the muleteer started the rabbits by his shouts. On approaching Argamasilla we followed the little canal which, with the Guadiana, makes the territory about the pueblo productive. Each little field taps the canal at a fixed hour and for a certain length of time, the amount of water taken being carefully measured and paid for accordingly. From Ezechiel's explanations, it was clear that the management of this complicated system of irrigation, perfect in spite of its primitiveness, is even to its details that which I had seen used in the oases of northern Africa. Here is, therefore, another one of those valuable legacies of the Moors against which one stumbles constantly in La Mancha.

V
El Toboso

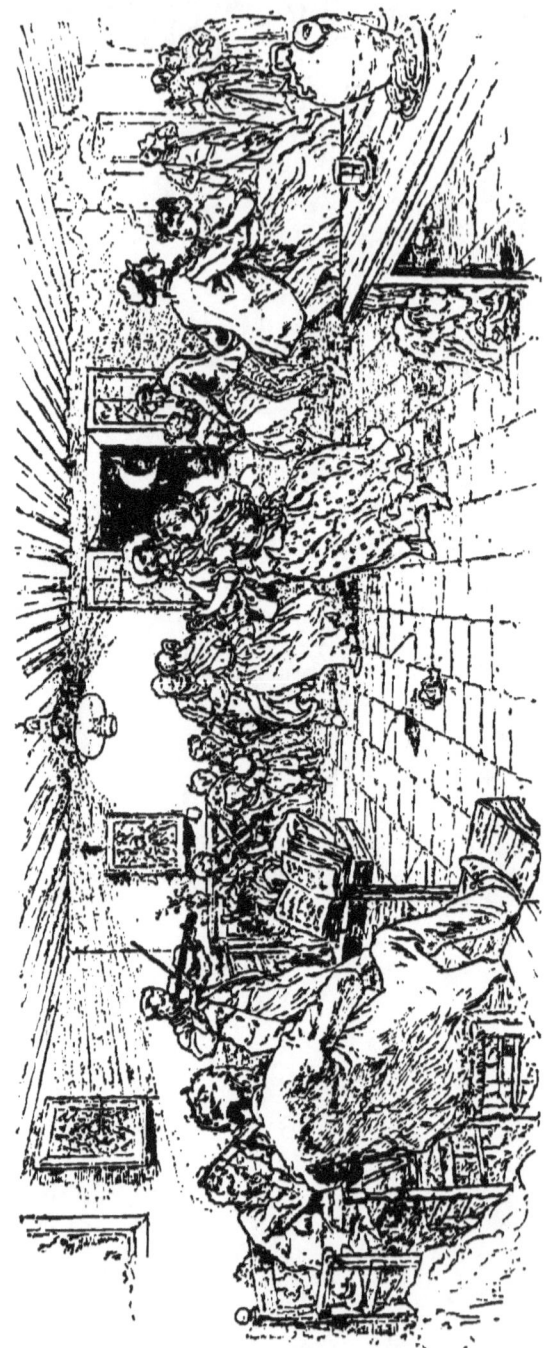

The Dance at Herencia.

El Toboso

STARTING from Argamasilla before daylight, our little mule had trudged during eight long hours the denuded, inhospitable plain of La Mancha, where the unchecked cold blasts from the Sierras hold wild riot in the winter, and which was now lying prostrate under the furious caresses of the sun ; her parched soil bursting now and again with dull sounds like the moans of a creature in pain. When we became aware of the proximity of the highway we were looking for, it was by some ruins, inevitable concomitants of this Land of the Dead. Before these silent, melancholy remains and in the absence of the living, one can but feel the presence of the dead. 'Tis as if the past centuries were walking by the side of the traveller, keeping him company, and little imagination is needed to people again this great artery of human communications, thrown across the undefiled country by the Romans, with Iberians, Goths, and Moors, with Spaniards of the time when Spain was the most powerful country of the civilized world, and see Isabella, Charles V., the sombre Philip, speeding on in all the splendid paraphernalia of royalty, and with their retinue of haughty Castilians. What a sense of the swing of history one has in such places, and before the eternity of nature how ephemeral and inconsequential human life seems. Ezechiel brings back some echoes of a past of which he is ignorant, in calling this road *arrecife*, the Arab name which has remained in the Manchegan dialect, one of the many patent souvenirs of five centuries of Moorish domination.

The ruins were of an important Venta, such a caravanserai as was found every few leagues when all travelling and traffic between Madrid and Seville passed along this royal highway. If the ingenious surmises of the learned, who have industriously erected their ponderous commentaries all around Cervantes's romance, are true, this Venta had the rare good fortune of being visited by Don Quixote in the beginning of his wanderings. It is there, in the court-yard now empty and deserted, that the Knight of the

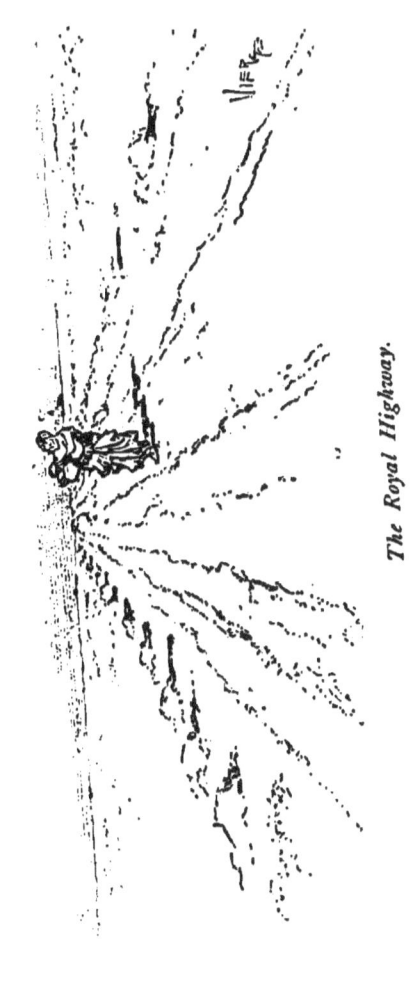

The Royal Highway.

Rueful Countenance kept his nocturnal vigil-at-arms preceding that morning when the rowdy, canny innkeeper made him a knight. To me let it be only what it surely is, and that is enough—one of the rare pages of the days of old, the mute witness of the comedies and tragedies, of the pleasures and troubles of some of our predecessors in the human procession. The advent of great personages, setting in a flutter inn-keeper and servants, and remembered and retold for many years; the merry and the sad reunions, the rogueries, picaresque incidents, are blotted out of our world. Only these crumbling walls remain, pegs on which the mind in passing hangs its imaginings of forgotten people. And how soon these last vestiges of the Venta shall fall, submerged in the inevitable tide of oblivion! Poor humanity, whose futile scratchings on the bosom of Mother Earth are but the making of its grave.

Finding the well empty, we resume our journey toward the road guard-house, two miles away, to find it closed, and on northward again, over the white road ablaze in the furnace heat. Under the cart-covering the scorching sun-rays liquefy one's brain; the

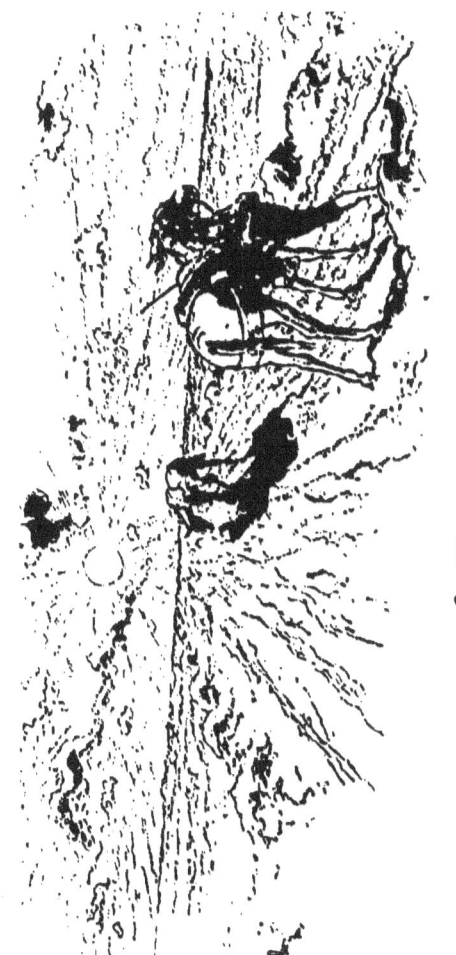

On The Royal Highway.

El Toboso

landscape around shimmers under the same trembling of the atmosphere that I had seen in the Sahara. Some olive-trees with their fantastic trunks and branches gnarled and crooked seem the vivid personifications of the tortures of the heat. A mendicant, seated in the dust scratching himself, is the first man we see on this royal road. Later two men pass us. " Poor ones also," says Ezechiel. Queer fashion for mendicants to carry their guns on their shoulders! But then it is a general custom in La Mancha. These two fellows look like opera supernumeraries, ex-

cept that their bronzed heads are finely chiselled and full of character, and that they are ragged beyond any possible imagination.

We attempt a hasty lunch in the shadow

El Toboso

of our cart, into which also the poor mule, lying down, stretches her head for comfort. It is hard work to eat without drinking, but such an experience has its value for the future enjoyment of that commonplace of life—the drinking of a glass of water.

Toward four in the afternoon we find another guard-house and pure cool water. What a pleasure it is to see the dulness leave the eyes of our mule while she drinks in long-measured draughts, her legs and neck bracing up, her whole countenance changed —alert now, ready for fresh exertions. The brave brute!

Across country again through a *vega*, a meadow where from the tall reeds, out of which baskets are made, pop out, like strange flowers, the heads of young horses and mules standing still, in herds, with their feet in the water of our friend the Guadiana.

Then the road leading up hill after hill, we alight and literally put our shoulders to the wheel. The character of the country changes. Climbing the first spurs of the mountains which form the northern limit of the plains of La Mancha, we enter one of the richest agricultural districts of Spain. Yet at this time of the year there is no sign of vegetation. The bare earth alone greets the eye in desolate hills, all cut up with ravines caused by the spring floods.

It is night and ten o'clock, when we reach Herencia, having travelled some fifty miles during the day, mostly on bad roads.

The inn with its sign, a wooden cross, dangling above the door, was a grand place after the hardships of the day. And as the Venta de Quesada which we had seen in the morning loomed up before Don Quixote's vision as a "castle with four towers, and spires of shining silver not wanting, drawbridge and moats, and all the appurtenances with which such places are painted." So to my mind appeared the little inn and its possibilities.

But whereas a drove of hogs greeted the chevalier, we found an interesting band of revellers. In honor of the feast-day upon which we had happened to stumble unawares, some thirty men were assembled round a huge table in the little courtyard, dimly and whimsically lighted by the dancing flames of some hanging lamps which though modern were roughly made by hand and of

El Toboso

an ancient model, the same as of those lamps of Roman decadent style found in Pompeii. These men were energetically at work getting through a Homeric feast, where, I learned afterward, some fifty pounds of beef, thirty of bread, and dozens of chickens were disposed of in the good old fashion and

The Plaza at Herencia.

El Toboso

washed down with wine *ad libitum*. The scene had an unusual fascination in that the participants were silent as if the affair were purely a matter of business. It proved to be the dinner offered once a year, in accordance with an ancient custom transmitted unbroken, by some rich proprietor to his dependants and the *arrieros* of his estate. Ezechiel informed me that the sturdy fellows had prepared themselves for the event by an unusually scant diet, as was evident by their going through their work like well oiled machines.

We fared finely ourselves over that peninsular dish—the rabbit—the animal found on the ancient coins of the country and testifying to the culinary gratitude of people not too spoiled in these matters. After our dinner I would have done the rabbit a like honor had I had the choosing of coin designs.

There was a dance afterward—very dignified—a mixed affair—local, with a dash of civilized notions thrown in, a delightfully clumsy mixture of the provincial and the civilized dance.

It was as if while attempting to disport

El Toboso

himself after our own fashion, a half peasant, half Moor, had been unable to divest himself of the ways that had become the most rigid parts of his nature. In such way the polka was half a cachucha, half a bolero, and the waltz smacked of the zapatera with its queer contortions of the torso, and the rhythmic beat of heels and toes.

But alas, Herencia was the most important place I had as yet come across in my Manchegan rambles, and the most disagreeable sign of its thrift and prosperity—the men dressed in the universal civilized garb that I met with on all sides while following the stream of people toward the sanctuary, where

El Toboso

was being celebrated the feast of Sant' Iago, the patron saint of Spain, "Don Saint James, the Moorslayer, one of the most valiant Saints and Knights of the squadrons of Christ—that ever the world had and Heaven has now" (Don Quixote, Part II., Chapter LVIII.). Near the entrance of the church, on a little table covered with a napkin, was a large platter full of coins. Its keeper, an old

El Toboso

lady, the traditional duenna, sunk in a low chair, and lost in the folds of her mantilla, kept fluttering her fan vigorously and at intervals, interrupting her constant mumbling of prayers, she turned to the next person to say, "Jesus, it's hot!" My little contribution is gracefully acknowledged in that way.

From the church door a company of soldiers lined the way to the altar, resplendent with its hundreds of lighted candles shining on pictures and marble columns, and cande-

El Toboso

labra and the profusion of gaudy paper flowers set in huge vases.

The low murmur of prayers grows louder and quieter with the faint suggestion of a rhythm, that of a national tune.

In a side chapel, before an old painting black with age and bright with real jewels, some silver ornaments, a gold diadem and bracelets glued on the canvas, a crowd of women on their knees form a picture à la Ribera, with beautiful oppositions of intense light and black shadows. While all heads are devoutly bowed, a single profile, straight and hard, remains erect—that of a young girl of the pure Arab type, with the large black eyes full of flame and shadows, with full lips firmly and finely drawn and sunk in the corners. A strangely sensuous face which, in a haughty way, in the consciousness, perhaps, of superb animality, seemed to wonder what the scene before it might have to do with real life. Why should that single figure, seemingly out of keeping with its environment, appear to me the most typical one? Perhaps because of the idiosyncrasies of my Don Quixote self and, I think, perhaps also because it was the one sincere, in-

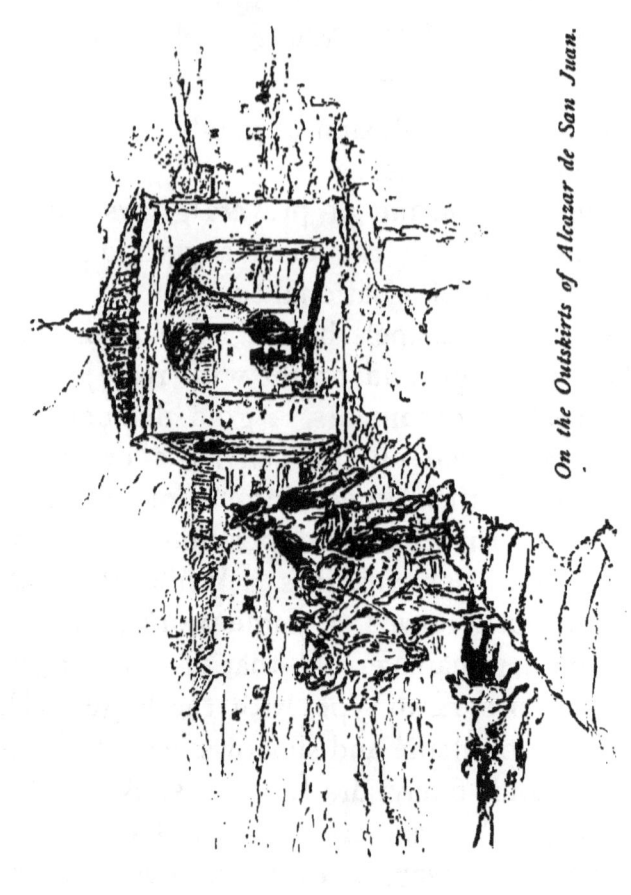

On the Outskirts of Alcazar de San Juan.

El Toboso

voluntary expression there of these Southern natures, which, having no deeply religious feelings, take life after a manner eminently practical. She cast cold, disrespectful glances toward the devout paraphernalia on the chapel walls, bringing to mind the levity with which in the age of the Inquisition Cervantes spoke of such things : " These tombs in which the bodies are of these great lords, have they silver lamps in front of them, or are the walls of their chapels adorned with crutches, grave clothes, periwigs, legs and eyes of wax, . . . ?" says Sancho in Don Quixote, Part II., Chapter VIII. It is a far cry from the peasant's disregard to the liberal indifference of a great Churchman. Yet under his hood the intellectual face of Cervantes's powerful friend, Archbishop Sandoval, Inquisitor-General, must have worn a quizzical smile at the audacity of that book and author he so authoritatively protected—otherwise the one might have ended in an *auto da fé*, and the other in a dungeon.

The sky is studded with an infinitude of stars. The streets are dark but for the few lights of some stands where fruit, bread, pastry, and the omnipresent *garbanzos* (chick

peas) are sold. The people are orderly, moving so quietly that one misses the exuberance of feeling, the bursts of merriment of the Italians on such occasions. No motions are made which would disturb the dignified folds of their capes and mantillas. Few words are exchanged, yet one catches snatches of those sententious Castilian proverbs, full of sap and sense, which are too near the seriousness of life to bring a laugh.

In the City Hall Tower, Alcazar de San Juan.

The Mills of Crijilano.

El Toboso

Two young men strolling about the groups pause; at a few twangs of their guitar the silent crowd presses around them. The two players face one another. One plays the accompaniment, the other, with that astonishing natural virtuosity which mimics real talent so well that one must know much to detect the difference, plays the air. Their poses are characteristic—the virtuoso standing straight, his head thrown back, the accompanist with bent body resting on one foot and his eyes riveted on his partner's guitar. When the song is finished a few low claps of appreciation are heard while the crowds noiselessly disperse.

But in the distance a louder, sensuous voice sings a *Malagueña*, which the wild expressive twangs of the guitar punctuate. There is fury in the accompaniment, passion in the voice, and this reveals another side of these people's natures—the smouldering fire under the ashes.

As we come out of the pueblo in the early morning a street merchant is already at work near the market-place, offering his stock of goods at auction to the country folks, the pilgrims, who are getting ready to return home. It is the one occasion for most of those who come to town but once a twelvemonth, on such a feast day, to make their necessary purchases for the whole year. And this peculiar demand has brought out a class of "drummers," whose life is spent in moving over the country, from *fiesta to fiesta.*

Reaching the highway outside the town, there goes before us a troop of chattering pilgrims, solid little women bedizened with bright kerchiefs on heads and shoulders, mounted a-top of the loads on their little donkeys. The dust clouds, glorified by the rising sun, make a halo about the gay picture full of movement.

We pass them, look back, and lo! the charm has vanished. The cavalcade is as commonplace as possible. It was the sun alone which made the pretty picture.

As we now turn to look at the receding town, its silhouette clear on the tawny curtain of the Sierras behind, it takes the bewitching appearance of a fresh and dainty vision in white garb, softened and beautified by the tender light of the morning. In regard to beauty, Spain is the democratic land

One of the Ancient Mills at Crijitano.

Near Crijitano.

El Toboso

par excellence. Decrepit buildings, half-ruined villages, ragged mendicants, have their daily hour of unrivalled splendor. Dilapidated objects and commonplace scenes touched by the sun of the south are turned by this incomparable magician into visions of loveliness. In the course of the day the glorious light dwells on each detail of the landscape, in turn giving it inexpressible charm and beauty, and leaving it a dull corpse whose life has departed.

And as we go on our journey this calm morning, there goes also with us in the gutters on each side of the well-kept road a

stream of fireworks—tiny blue flowers, which against the neutral background of parched grass and pierced by the slanting rays of the sun, are transfigured into radiant jewels.

All too soon do we come to Alcázar de San Juan, a town of some commercial importance since the railroad branch to Valencia joins here the main road from Madrid to Seville. Alcázar naturally boasts of its station with its "*buffet.*" But far from me is the desire to eat from a table covered with a table-cloth bearing the evidences of much service, Spanish imitations of English steaks, or to drink so-called Bordeaux wine from a glass, instead of black, rough Val de Peñas from a skin or earthenware bottle—and listen to the impossible Hispano-Franco-English talk of the waiter. There is enough local color left all around this buffet, symbol of nineteenth-century civilization, which, like a fungus amidst the grass and little plants of a prairie, is here stranded in provincial and old-time surroundings. We take a look at the adjacent country from the tower of the Town Hall, and have a hasty breakfast and rest at the fine *fonda*, whose monumental façade stands on a large plaza, the market-place, where an amusing spectacle is going on under the watchful eye of a municipal

In Crijitano.

El Toboso

employee armed with a short broom. In the brief intervals between his exchange of civilities and gossip with passers-by, he plays at sweeping the pavement with such lordly poses and measured movements as would befit a grandee, if such an one, which Heaven forbid, were sunk to so lowly a pastime. Market hour is over, but a few peasants still linger in the hope of disposing of their stock in trade that they have spread out in the dust on the pavements. They shout and sing the virtues of each particular fruit and vegetable, paying extravagant compliments to every housekeeper who comes on the scene or poking fun at one another, grumbling at Providence and bad luck, all in a jolly spirit, and with rough, strong voices and ripples of laughter. There are some women among them, handsome, in multi-colored dresses, and it is of one of them that we buy our provision of fruit. "*Vaya usted con Dios.*" "God be with you," she says as I leave. Then calling me back, "Caballero, when you go home tell your girl that they are pretty fine women, the women of Alcázar. Good in business, and good in love, and mind you, Señor, they love but once!"

El Toboso

Sitting on a bench under the entranceway of the inn—the largest we have as yet seen—I get an idea of what such a place as the Venta de Cardenas, or that of Quesada, may have been in the old days. In spite of the inevitable dirt and slovenliness, the place has an unmistakable *cachet* of prosperity,

and the cheery innkeeper and her helpers move about busily. In front of us some female servants are sewing, repairing sheets,

fashioning garments for the master's help. A buffoon's sole occupation is to sweep the floor, while a colleague goes after him sprinkling it the whole day long. The big, fat *ama*, with a face like a Roman senator, strides all over the place, keeping a watchful eye on details, and giving imperative orders in a voice which sounds like a clarion blast. The *amo*, with bunch of keys dangling from his belt, sees to the filling of wine-bottles, to the killing of poultry, to the cutting of meat. The cooks—at work under our eyes—are two

El Toboso

old witches, who alternately disappear and reappear in the smoke of the wood fire. The *ama*, who, in spite of her bulk, is here, there, everywhere at once, comes up behind them, often unexpectedly snatching stewpans, tasting the food, adding ingredients, and upbraiding the witches in the grandest style, with that magnificent organ aforementioned. However, the real ruler of this *fonda* appears to be a spoiled little boy, hardly three years old, precocious and saucy—the Benjamin of the large family. He keeps

On the Plaza, Crijitano.

El Toboso

his special *criada* busy—a handsome young woman, in orange skirt, red stockings, and black shoes (oh, luxury!), who looks the picture of helplessness, when, blushing prettily, she casts frightened glances toward the *ama* at every fresh evidence of the little rogue's mischievous spirit.

Alcázar de San Juan and its *fonda* having passed out of sight were nothing more to me than one of the souvenirs of my journey added to the others—a sharp negative, indelibly preserved in the camera of my brain—when we caught sight of the windmills of the Campo de Crijitano, one of which, it is said, our knight met with in his celebrated adventure. Poor Quixote does not seem so mad after all when one first sees this row of mills set irregularly on the crest of a hill and looking like nothing one has ever seen, more like a collection of queer, primitive toys stuck there by the weird caprice of a lunatic. As one approaches and views them one by one, these clumsy-looking affairs, propped up like very aged persons, are thoroughly fantastic. No wonder the worthy knight mistook them for giants! On his native soil Cervantes's book takes an

El Toboso

added pungency. How much it is of the country, how true to life are the characters, descriptions and language, one needs to live here among the people to know. There is a great charm in stumbling at all instants on things it has made familiar to us. For example, not only do the inhabitants of certain villages of La Mancha dress to-day like Sancho Panza, but all Manchegans are mines of those old sayings in which the wisdom of generations is crystallized into proverbs which, like him, they constantly use to sum up tersely a situation.

Near these mills we stop to inquire of a water-cart driver our shortest way to the pueblo. Ezechiel got the desired informa-

El Toboso

tion, and then " Brother," he said, " it is water you are carrying ? "

" Fine drinking - water, yea. Don't you want some ? "

" Thanks, no ; our bottle is half full, still."

"*Cascara!* It must be hot, have some of mine," answered the man.

Our bottle is filled with sweet fresh water, and Ezechiel calls the man, who is going back to his cart :

" Here, here's a pataquilla " (a cent), " and we are obliged to you."

" No, brother, I don't want any money, I am glad to give you good water, that's all."

" But we all have to live by our labor, and

El Toboso

you have to drive many miles to get that water."

"*Bueno*, but it's better to make a friend than to make ten dollars," then, catching a glimpse of me: "All right, brother," he says to Ezechiel, "I see the caballero can better afford to give this money than I to be without it, and so I'll take the money."

I buttered the pataquilla with a cigarette, and added the valued courtesy of offering him light from my cigar. He stood caressing our mule while giving us again instructions as to our road. Under the scant protection of a handkerchief, wound turban-like around his head, his fine brown face was aglow in the sunlight, and the blood gave a flamboyant hue to his firm cheeks like the rich color of a hard red apple. His black eyes flashed and the veins of his neck and forehead bulged out; he was the picture of a superbly healthy, careless, happy creature.

After he had gone Ezechiel said, sententiously: "That pataquilla won't do him any good, señor, for *para dar y tener, seso es menester*." To give or to keep hath need of brains. "He'll drink or smoke it as soon as he reaches the village."

El Toboso

Campo de Crijitano, named for the productive land, the rich fields around it (campo-field), is one of the three or four rare specimens of the best Manchegan pueblos. In spite of its well-to-do air, of its big houses, some of which have glass windows, stone carvings and ornaments of wrought iron, it preserves as strong a local flavor as its humbler sisters. Being fortunately removed from the railroad, it remains, in spite of its prosperity, an old-time community. Having variety in its picturesqueness and dignity in many of its buildings, it is good to find it Manchegan to the core, in nowise different from the poorest villages of this land of enchantment where the old costumes, habits and old houses have remained unchanged for ages, for centuries.

The Campo is dozing when at high noon we meander through its precipitous street toward the posada. Quevedo alone, the master *par excellence* of picaresque descriptions, could have done justice to the types we find there. The fellow who stood at the door with a bandage around his head which he sprinkles with some old woman's ointment kept in a greasy pig-skin vessel, the infirm

In Toboso.

El Toboso

amo and *ama*, each greater, surely, in breadth than in height; the collection of half-naked hangers on escaped from nowhere but the pages of "Pablo de Segovia, The Great Ruffian." The dingy interior—parlor, dining, sleeping-room. What was it? or, rather,

what was it not? with its indescribable dinginess, filth, and flies, is a place not to be de-

A Glimpse of the Big Church, Toboso.

El Toboso

scribed. But there we had to rest under the slanting, low roof with its roughly hewed beams, cobwebbed all over. In choosing our place we pass by or walk over muleteers, pedlers, swine-herds, stretched on the bare floor. On the walls harnesses and sombreros are hanging on nails, in the corners are sacks of grain, packages, wine-skins belonging to the sleepers, and guarded by little curs that snarl silently when one gets too near, and would bark and bite at the slightest attempt to touch their masters' property.

In the weird light—a half-light—what a fine picture this interior makes! Two stables are near us— one for the mules, the other for the pigs. These last are grunting, the mules kick, and lean cats, prowling about in their search for food, mew. A mule chased from the stable picks her way quickly among the snoring sleepers, not one of whom moves, while her master, trudging behind with the harness, urges her on with a peculiar noisy shout ending in a hiss. No interruptions wake these sleepers whose slumbers are deep when chance favors them in the twenty-four hours—four-fifths of which are spent in labor. Resting until the last minute, they are up and

El Toboso

at work in an instant. There is no stretching of the limbs, no washing to be gone through, no clothes to put on. A drink of water and they are behind their mules under the broiling sun, the crooked stick in their hands, wide awake and singing.

We start at three in the afternoon, harnessing the mule in the midst of a drove of pigs—a hundred or more—the village pigs, which are being gathered together to go to the fields under the guardianship of boys. After following a beautiful road for a league or more and passing the sanctuary on the hill where reposes the miraculous image of the patron saint of the Campo, " Our Lady of Crijitano," we strike across wheat-fields and in a couple of hours reach the barren country, sparsely dotted with clusters of trees, where Don Quixote met with one of his most pitiful adventures, the first sight of his lady Dulcinea changed by malefic enchantment into a coarse peasant wench.

Quite melancholy are the approaches of Toboso, whose few houses, built largely of sculptured fragments of ancient important structures, plainly tell the decadence of the renowned and prosperous city which accord-

Guardias Civiles Making an Investigation at Toboso.

ing to an official report had nine hundred houses in the reign of Philip II. There is nevertheless a winning charm, a sort of dignity to the place like that of a deserving unfortunate who preserves some gentlemanly demeanor.

Its dilapidated houses, strewn around two stern, forbidding-looking churches, appeared, in spite of their scars, clean and well kept. Its ravine-like lanes were free from the noxious sights which had grown so familiar to me as inseparable adjuncts of Manchegan streets. In Toboso I also found that exotic wonder an exquisitely clean posada. It was late when we saw it, and I hardly dared trust my first impression, but it stood the test of a detailed survey in the full light of the next day. Imagine Dutch cleanliness in La Mancha; floors of court-yards and rooms shining, barren of dust, curtains at the little windows, mats at the doors, and in appropriate places on the white walls pathetic attempts at decoration in the shape of religious prints set in colored paper frames!

Pieces of furniture, chairs, chests, and tables, curiously carved, and the array of brass

El Toboso

bowls, spoons, and ladles of quaint and rough design in the kitchen were beautifully polished. But there were no servants in this poor inn. The family—father, mother, and two daughters—kept the place in order. The women were dignified and kindly, and as they went about their work in the house an atmosphere of gentility hovered around them. Their simple manners, devoid neither of repose nor of grace, were pleasant to watch. And then looking clean and neat they made me feel less far from home.

The father, a six-foot man of about fifty, with huge frame, big shoulders, clean face, and a peculiarly low forehead, spent his time alternately in giving orders and praying. On our arrival we found the family finishing supper, and before our inquiries were answered the four creatures stood with heads bowed low down on the table, chanting an interminable litany, and kept us waiting until the long ordeal was at an end. As soon as we could make our wishes known the women, excited and fluttered at the advent of guests, disappeared to go and prepare our supper, when the father straightway started on his hobby—religion. He was a fanatic, with the fierce intolerance which is usually considered by foreigners one of the strong traits of the Spaniards. I must say that, until now, I had seen nothing of intolerance among the Manchegans; but this man more than made up for it. Don Quixote discussing chivalry was no more enthusiastic, not a whit less hare-brained than this giant inn-

El Toboso

keeper when inveighing against the bad ways of the present generation, against its indifference to church attendance, its non-observance of religious practices—in short, its lack of what was formerly termed the religious spirit in Spain. He would illustrate his ideas by quotations from theological books, cross himself when pronouncing the name of God or the saints, and he would occasionally break in upon his reasonings to ask us our

opinions of some prayers to be used on special occasions of temptation and illness which he had selected from the old manuals

In the Posada's Courtyard, Toboso.

El Toboso

of piety. This world was going the way of the tempter, was the burden of his song, and he pointed to the fact that in the last century every other house in Toboso was a church, a private chapel, or a convent, while the Government having taken away lands and fields and convents from monks and sisters, there were hardly any monks or sisters left, and only two churches. He remembered how beautiful were the holy services he used to attend in his youth, with the magnificent tapestries, gold and silver vases, and rich ornaments which made the altars like visions of paradise. " All these riches had to be sold, little by little, and thus the church was now bereft of her power for good."

Ezechiel's opinion of our host was expressed figuratively in a Sancho-like fashion, made more contemptuous by a shrug of the shoulders : "Well, señor, he talks, like a linnet, out of a mighty small head."

A sad lot was that of the women of the house with such a master. He meant well, of course, but his was an iron will, and everyone must agree with the spirit of his doctrine as well as with his minute observances. Thus

El Toboso

Maria and Juana, the daughters, in passing before each saintly image—each prayer cut from the pages of ancient missals, adorning the walls all over the house, in their little frames ingeniously fashioned of straw and gilt paper—had to bow and stop, audibly reciting a pious ejaculation. While in the midst of their work, the hands of the giant would beckon, and business had to be instantly abandoned for the recitation of some special prayer for the deliverance of slaves or the conversion of the faithless. Guests were less fortunate than the cat and dog, the only inmates enjoying full liberty in the house. There was no escape possible from the tyrannical ways of this singular *amo*, who, caring little about the things of this world, would let his guests starve or go away without paying if only he could improve the opportunity to make them religious after his own heart.

That was the reason for the lack of patronage of this otherwise admirable place. When in the evening, seated outdoors and hearing songs of merriment in the neighborhood, we wondered what was going on, "It is from the other posada," said the *amo*. "May

Maria.

El Toboso

God burn it to the ground, for devil-possessed people run it and idolaters alone frequent it."

Of the rough and brutal character, proverbial in Cervantes's time, of the inhabitants of Toboso, Morisco refugees from Granada, who had not had time to outlive the rude, fierce traits of their Arab ancestors, I saw no trace. But the sole industry of the town now as then is the manufacture of large jars, *tinajas*, made of the tufous earth which abounds in the locality and the Tobosan tinajas with their graceful swelling lines and curves are still renowned in the Castiles. The principal church is the same one Cervantes described, and the blind alley where the roguish squire insisted that the princely castle of the fair damsel was, still exists. I could not miss the opportunity of walking wide awake into the romancer's dream, "while the village was wrapt in silence, for all the inhabitants were asleep—reposing at full stretch—as they say," and with Don Quixote and Sancho pass in the shadow cast by the "great pile" and, looking at the belfry tower, remark with Sancho that the pile was a church and not a palace. The scene was just like

El Toboso

that of the book. "No sound was heard but the barking of dogs which stunned Don Quixote's ears and troubled Sancho's heart. Now and then a jackass brayed, pigs grunted, and cats mewed, whose voices of various sound were heightened in the silence of the night."

El Toboso

We start at midnight on our return journey to Argamasilla, passing the Campo de

Crijitano before daybreak and going down the slopes to the meadows of the Guadiana, and cross the river on a bridge whose length shows what mighty proportions this puny stream is wont to assume during the rainy season. Toward noon we come to a *quinteria* (large farm) and Ezechiel goes

Juana.

El Toboso

in to ask permission to enter, a privilege never refused but which must be asked for and granted, like everything else in this country, with the elaborately polite formulas sanctioned by custom. Our cart enters the square spacious courtyard, with low buildings on two sides and walls on the others. We find a hearty welcome in the kitchen, where eight field-laborers, with the inevitable long blades in their hands, are sitting on low stools energetically discussing the contents of a big soup-pot, the national *puchero*. The cook, a bashful young woman, who blushes prettily on the slightest provocation, makes a good contrast to these dark-skinned, muscular men, who, teasing one another in a good-natured way, seem to have the best time in the world. At the entrance-door a band of famished cats and dogs, too well trained to dare to approach, look on with flaming eyes, uttering half-suppressed whines. Everyone treats us with extreme courtesy and kindness, and I doubt if in any other country the stranger could find such manners and such tact among a set of low laborers like this. After lunch I was shown into a little whitewashed room, dark and cool,

Picking the Saffron Flowers.

where over a stone bench a couch of mats had been arranged, and I was left alone for a much-needed bit of siesta.

As it was harvest-time the place was lively, but most of the year the *casero* (farmer, or rather guardian of the farm) is alone with the dogs and his Winchester, and the large gates being closed, the *quinteria* becomes a fortress. The *casero* then does patrol-duty to prevent damage to the fields and possible raids against the stores of grain, provisions, and wine. In lonely places such as these, *caseros* have an exciting life, and few of them are there who reach an old age. This one thinks the game worth the candle. "It is a fine life, sir," he tells me, while caressing his Winchester; "plenty to eat and drink, some money besides, and then a chance to use one's gun."

After the siesta we resume our journey over the familiar plain, where, far away before us, our goal appears as a faint mirage. Argamasilla impresses one differently as one approaches it from some new direction. Now it looks like an Oriental city, with its brilliant white walls set at the end of an alameda, a long oasis of grand poplars with

The Laborers Lunch at Harvest-time on a Quinteria.

El Toboso

an undergrowth of fig and lemon trees. The whole picture has the color of the Orient, the same sky, the same warm purple haze over the horizon, and the plain is as flat and tawny as the desert; the poplars alone are out of place, and palm-trees are lacking to make the likeness complete.

VI
The Morena

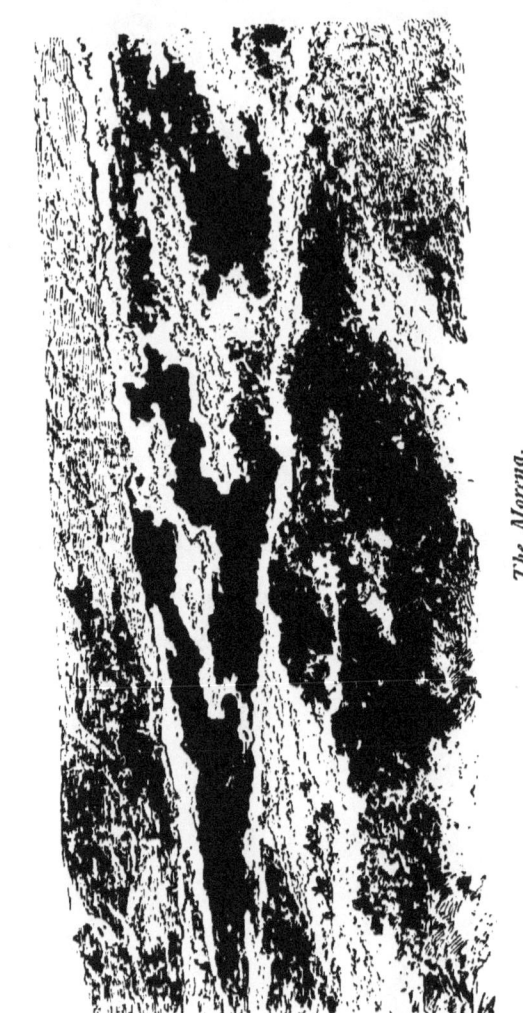

The Morna.

The Morena

THE trip to the Sierra Morena was my sole infidelity to Ezechiel. On the eve of departure from Argamasilla we had an interview that is likely to remain one of my rarest recollections. It was my last dinner at the Posada del Carmen, where, as the honored guest, Ezechiel behaved with his usual dignity and tact, his gentle voice adding charm to his words.

The meal over, we walked across the way to the one shop of the place, whose meagre stock of cotton goods was displayed in a low room no larger than six by ten feet, that, in order to settle my accounts with him, I might get change for a Spanish bank-note. I counted the number of *douros*, each one of which was the equivalent of a day of his services and those of his conveyance, and gave

The Morena

them to him with the addition of an extra compensation.

The good man counted the pieces carefully again and again, looked puzzled, and finally called my attention to the mistake made in giving him more than his due. Whereupon explaining that it was intentional and that I wished I could make it more, I asked him to accept the little gift as a small acknowledgment of his loyal services. He continued to look embarrassed, but finally thanked me for my kindness and went away. An hour after, he returned with the extra compensation. "No, Señor," he said, "I can't take this. We made our price. It was more than I usually get, and as this job was an easy one, I am the gainer. We stand quits, and I could not think well of myself nor would you think as kindly of me if I were to take your gift."

"But, man, I consider you have earned it by the money you saved me in your purchases at the posadas."

"That was the bargain, Señor. No, you must take this back. Let me shake hands with you as with a friend, and God be with you and yours."

The Morena

I deplored the necessity which deprived me of his faithful attendance, but his little mule could not have made the long, arduous journey to and from the Morena without taking much more time than I had at my disposal. There are such incidents in one's happiest experiences, and this loss of Ezechiel's companionship I could not help feeling keenly as the premonition of the humdrum days of civilized routine that were to follow my last excursion into La Mancha. It was unreasonable, of course, for journeys like these derive their interest from the contrast they make to one's ordinary manner of life.

I had no other course but to go by rail into the very heart of the mountains, and

The Morena

thereby make what I thought would prove a prosaic and hardly pleasant beginning. But the train crept along so slowly and made so long a stop at every little settlement that the novel experience of being able to examine at leisure all details of the landscape proved rather enjoyable. 'Twas not in the least like the car-travelling we are accustomed to, but rather like the progress of a mule or a horse going at a brisk pace.

At first the flat country had the familiar parched and dreary look, then, as we went along, the vineyards invaded it and soon filled the plain in an unbroken mass as far as the eye could reach.

We passed through the most famous wine-producing district in Spain. The prosperous town which gives it its name Valdepeñas (Valley of Stones) had; in spite of its commercial importance, the same tiled-roof houses scattered around a big church, which are so characteristic of Manchegan villages. It had an unexpected contrast in the shape of some spick and span modern-looking bodegas (distilleries and wine emporiums) with their names printed in black letters three feet high on their dazzling white walls.

The Morena

I suffered from the incongruity of seeing this blatant signature of our civilization in so primitive a place, and found it particularly disagreeable to be so bluntly reminded of home.

Everywhere from the Manchegan plains the serrated outline on the southern horizon serves as a weather bureau. It is the Morena. We had been approaching it gradually, though it seemed always out of reach. After leaving the Valdepeñas region the character of the country changed, becoming more and more denuded and rocky, and the denticulated Sierra Morena I had become familiar with was lost to sight.

The Morena

Having left behind the yellow and purple immensity of the plain, fading away like a hazy sea, we found ourselves, on ascending the first high spur, encircled by mountains. Our path became steeper, rocky slopes being piled one upon another until, after a succession of curves and steep grades, the train stopped and panted for breath at the station of Almuradiel.

Alighting with my scant luggage tied to a crooked staff, I happened by lucky accident on old José and his antediluvian mule and cart, rigged together with broken harness and pieces of rope, rotten from long service. Without waste of words a bargain was made and off we went toward the village of Viso del Marques, the most convenient headquarters for an exploration of the mountainous recesses, where some of the strangest and most wonderful adventures befell our friends of the Book.

What a delight it was to be on such an errand bent in these weird and bleak surroundings of romance, with the sun shining fiercely and a cold wind blowing half a gale, while fingering, so to speak, the interesting book of José's wisdom by means of leading

The Morena

questions concerning himself, the people, the country, snatching thus inevitable bits of familiar history clothed in queer garb, yet nevertheless recognizable. Wizen-faced José, who had seen eighty winters and improved his opportunities, could put a lot of sense and shrewd knowledge into his entertaining talk.

We proceeded at a snail's pace on a terrible road, that hardly scratched the rocky soil of a bleak plateau. A fin-like barrier of sharp, serrated mountains rose before us, and on our side toward the south. Between and above these nearer peaks others appeared, and in the distance two higher summits, rather faint, raised their lordly heads. In this savagely lonely and imposing ensemble there were here and there, in the ridges of the plateau, some fields of vines and wheat accentuating its barrenness. And a few vigorous plants, dwarfed by the constant struggle against the elements and holding to the live rock with hardy roots resembling claws, managed to brace themselves in the crevices and stubbornly resist the north wind's riotous blasts.

Against the same enemy Viso del Marques

huddled its solid, low houses in a compact mass, appearing at a distance so indistinguishable from its surroundings that only on getting nearer to its standard-bearer, the belfry tower, square and squatty, bulging out from amid the little, irregular cubes of masonry, did I recognize them, not as the natural accidents of the landscape, but as the abodes of a human community. I fancy this same mediæval tower must have heralded El Viso to Don Quixote and Sancho in their flight toward the mountain fastnesses after their deliverance of, and scuffle with, the gang of galley-slaves, or in the words of Cid Hamet Benengali's translator, "the several unfortunates who, much against their will, were being carried to where they had no wish to go."

Shouts, beating of drums, and confusing sounds, striking our ears in the lulls between the gusts of wind, proclaimed the fact that something unusual was going on in the village. By good fortune it chanced to be the yearly local fiesta, and in the main street, teeming with people, we found it not easy to proceed. Our aged steed started kicking before a brawny Asturian pedler of brass

The Morena

brazeros, who beat his wares with a stick the better to advertise them.

Booths and tables were surrounded by peasant-folk, whose serious, honest countenances appeared hypnotized by the lively talk of drummers and fakirs. The male inhabitants were sitting before their doorsteps enjoying the animated spectacle, while the windows blossomed with the swarthy faces of excited women. Children and dogs ran crazily every way, donkeys brayed, and in corners against the walls patient mules

The Morena

looked on through half-closed eyes, shrewd and critical.

At the Casa Teresa the sixty years' old Señora Teresa had a fetching air of gentility, which, however, did not disguise her keen sense of business. She satisfied herself in a few minutes of the desirability of permitting me to be her guest. She put it in a nice way, excluding the vulgarity of the word boarder, though there was no doubt from the enormity of her demand, a peseta (about eighteen cents) a day for the best room, that "guest" was her sugar-coating to a sharp pill. As they say in Spain: *Poderoso caballero Es Don Dinero. Dios es omnipotente Y el dinero es su teniente.* "A powerful gentleman is Lord Money. God is all powerful and Money is his lieutenant."

El Viso being dropped on the edge of the civilized world, with the Sierra and wilderness on the other side, and removed therefore from the track of travel, there are no accommodations for the rare travellers—no fondas nor posadas—and this house was the only one where the infrequent provincial or government employee coming for some specific work—usually a tour of inspection—could

The Morena

find shelter. It gratified the little busybody to be brought into relations with such important personages, and while I did not have the glamour of an official position about me, yet she was full of cordiality toward the rich one who could so readily throw away eighteen cents for mere shelter, when he might just as well have slept under the porch of some house or on a street corner and saved the precious money.

She proved to be a capital cook, and her house was kept so scrupulously neat that I considered it a privilege indeed to live in it.

And the way she ordered affairs, with the help of a little servant-girl, some twelve years old, whom she loved and who loved her, and managed her rather decorative husband — a caballero who did not stoop to work, but who was cuddled and made much of—was something delightful. There was as much shrewd humor, kindliness, and *naïveté* in the scenes these three people played be-

The Morena

fore me as in the most entertaining chapter of Quixote—enough to make the most melancholy bosom kindle with human sympathy. The small house was unique of its kind; Doña Teresa's strong personality was impressed upon everything in it, and in such a pronounced manner that to live in, or enter, it gave as novel a sensation as a first visit to a Japanese house might give.

As its inmates were kept indoors by sun in summer and snow in winter, the interior was made as attractive as possible, a home-like little world. There were cats, birds, and potted plants also—who ever would dream of finding potted plants in a Manchegan house!—more wonderful still, as in the suburban home of the Parisian *petit rentier*, there were vines, carefully trained and watched, and a pet pear-tree in the little courtyard between the divisions of the house, front and back.

In the front room were queerly shaped pieces of old furniture, connected by strips of matting over the spotless floor of hardened earth, and I soon learned that one must always walk in the middle of the strips, otherwise the house-keeper's distress was as painful to see as her efforts to conceal it. There were many odds and ends of quaint and curious brass things and bric-à-brac, which were to be looked at and talked about but not touched, and chairs not to be used

under any circumstances. In fact the favorite seats were a stone in the courtyard and the door-sill. In my room the beautiful old chest of drawers was inspected every time I went out, to see that it had not suffered injuries at my inexperienced hands, and my bed was polished till it shone like some rare old bronze.

The Morena

I could not understand how the old lady found time to keep everything in such perfect condition; to bargain at length and shrewdly over every cent she spent on the marketing, (by the way, the peasant tradesmen never were allowed to enter the sacred precincts of the house, all trading being done from the doorsteps); to cook dainty and complicated dishes; to pay constant attention to her husband and her little servant, caressingly tending the one and playing merrily with the other; and to be always ready for a chat with guest or neighbor. But she did it, and managed it all cheerily, graciously, with an omnipresent watchfulness for opportunities, an ever-alert eye to business.

We spent the two days of the fiesta— Teresa's husband and I — roaming about the streets, smoking cigarettes, meeting in turn most of the villagers and indulging in short conversations, the burden of which was, on the part of my new acquaintances, the beauty of the fiesta—the like of which had not been seen for many years. They were good representatives of mountaineers, people of few words, sound on things essential, and loving the comparative freedom of their seclusion from the rest of the world.

While enjoying the fiesta they looked with disfavor upon the foreign element, as they called it, of travelling merchants, who had invaded their village to sell the few simple things they needed—harnesses, potteries, kitchen utensils, cotton and woollen cloths, kerchiefs, and trinkets. There was no sympathy, no assimilation between them. It was like the attitude of society toward actors, here quite justified, for the strangers, riffraff of all provinces of Spain, were a tough set, crafty, trying to cheat wherever they could, but knowing also how to curb their impudence at any intimation that the temper of the buyer was aroused.

The bull-fight had been the attraction of the day before my arrival, not such a bull-fight as one sees in cities, but a purely local affair gotten up only when the flesh of the poor brute—the most ferocious animal of the village herds—is sold beforehand. Even the poorest have something to spend in view of such an event, in which everyone takes part, the bull-ring being the great courtyard of a neighboring mediæval castle. As a re-

The Morena

sult of this democratic slaughter, the man who succeeds in dealing the death-blow is looked upon as the village hero and followed the ensuing year by admiring eyes wherever he goes. I had the honor of meeting the butcher-boy who had just achieved this distinction, and found him fully aware of his importance.

Fortunately the temporary theatre, set

upon the public square, remained. Performances were given whenever an audience collected, attracted by the inducements vociferously shouted in a hoarse, husky voice by

Getting Ready for the Journey.

The Morena

the fellow who assumed the manifold duties of manager, actor, and, if not playwright, at least, adapter of plays. After the traditional custom, each piece opened with a prologue and ended with a string of jests and apologies to the audience; each personage coming or going without the slightest regard to the unfolding of the story, its possibilities, or limitations of time.

Theatre and performances can, in fact, be well described in the words of Cervantes, speaking of the dramatist Lope de Rueda :

" In the time of this celebrated Spaniard," says Cervantes, "the whole apparatus of a manager was contained in a large sack, and consisted of four white shepherd's jackets, turned up with leather, gilt and stamped ; four beards and false sets of hanging locks, and four shepherd's crooks, more or less. The plays were colloquies, like eclogues, between two or three shepherds and a shepherdess, fitted up and extended with two or three interludes, whose personages were sometimes a negress, sometimes a bully, sometimes a fool, and sometimes a Biscayan ; for all these four parts, and many others, Lope himself performed with the greatest excellence and skill that can be imagined. . . . The theatre was composed of four benches, arranged in a square, with five or six boards laid across them, that were thus raised about four palms from the ground. . . . The furniture of the theatre was an old blanket, drawn aside by two cords, making what they call the tiring-room, behind which were the musicians, who sang old ballads without a guitar."

Performances, then as now, occurred whenever an audience could be gathered, apparently both forenoon, afternoon, and evening, for at the end of one of his plays Lope invites his "hearers only to eat their dinners and return to the square and witness another." The most useful personage appeared to me to be the fool, who happened in at unexpected moments, usually when the attention of the audience waned, and was kicked and abused with bad words and blows for his stupid simplicity. The spectators were silent, laughing rarely, and looking upon the antics of the buffoon with extreme seriousness.

El Viso has a post of the Guardia Civile. The district being in large part impractica-

The Morena

ble for horses, these men radiating from headquarters here have to cover on foot some fifteen miles as the crow flies, in every direction. This profession is not a sinecure in the Morena. Guardias, alternating night with day work, are on patrol duty sixteen out of the twenty-four hours, the remaining being devoted to their families (all being married as a rule) and to needful rest. They are under an effective system which controls their movements even in remote and deserted places, and going always in pairs, are never sent twice in succession on the same route. All they receive for their

services is less than thirty cents of our money per day, out of which they pay for their clothes, food, lodging, etc.

I had presented my request for the neces-

The Morena

sary escort, without which it would not have been safe to make the excursion I had planned, and the morning after the festivities started at a brisk pace between two young Guardias, with Winchesters on their shoulders, who walked with the short Spanish military step, pretty but ineffective and grotesque compared with the long, swinging motion, bending low the knees, of the Swiss moun-

taineers. The Guardias' tight uniforms of heavy, dark cloth (alike in summer and winter) made them look clumsy and stiff as dressed-up doll soldiers, their heavily

The Morena

fringed black eyes and long twisted mustachios adding an element of make-believe fierceness such as one expects nowhere but in stageland.

We went up a slope, which, ending abruptly a short distance above, seemed to be surmounted by a sober mass of deep purple, the chain of summits forming the dorsal fin of the Sierras.

After that first impression we found ourselves going down and across desert ridges and spurs whose monotonous, tawny hide made the most effective of foregrounds to the great serrated mountains unveiled now

On the Road to Los Molinos.

The Morena

from base to summit, their shapes and scars blended into an harmonious medley of luminous colors—stepping-stones to the inexpressible radiance of the unbroken, deep azure above.

Our path went meandering downward over the sharp, live rock which cut into one's shoes, and as we advanced the rugged desolation of our surroundings made the airy and transparent curtain of the Sierras, growing in height before us, seem a mirage. It was the right time to call to mind the passage where Cervantes describes the knight's feelings in such a place as this:

"And as they entred in farther among those mountaines, we cannot recount the joy of our Knight, to whom those places seemed most accommodate to atchieve the adventures he searched for. They reduced to his memory the marvellous accidents that had befalne Knights Errant in like solitudes and desarts: and he rode so overwhelmed and transported by these thoughts, as he remembred nothing else. Nor Sancho had any other care (after he was out of feare to be taken) but how to fill his belly with some of these relikes which yet remained of the

The Morena

Clericall spoyles; and so hee followed his lord, taking now and then out of a basket (which Rozinante carried for want of the Asse) some meat, lining therewithall his paunch; and whilst he went thus imployed, he would not have given a mite to encounter any other adventure how honourable soever." (Part I, Chapter XXIII., THOMAS SHELTON'S TRANSLATION.)

Like Sancho, our companions and guests, Doña Teresa, her husband, and her little maid-servant, who were following us in José's cart, whiled the time away by eating greased *bañuelos* * and drinking the powerful Valdepeñas—a combination which made them superbly oblivious to jolting and heat. And ever and anon, the irrepressible flow of their high spirits burst forth into extemporaneous and hurriedly recited litanies, ending in long, piercing notes, and celebrating the giver of the feast, the beauty of the day, and the joy of their hearts.

One loses all sense of direction in these chaotic wastes, peopled only by flocks of

---

* A fried pasty without any filling, which is the dainty breakfast dish in well-to-do families of Southern Spain and among the Moors of Northern Africa.

The Morena

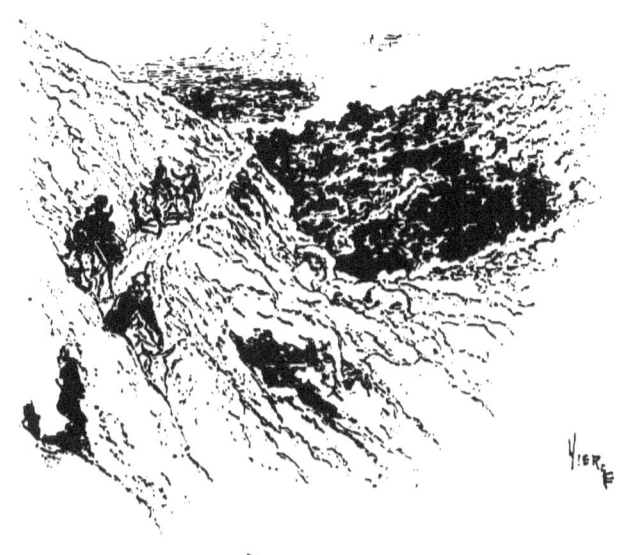

hills pressing around and filling the horizon on three sides with strange and varied forms. The heat is stifling in these closed gulleys, and it was only when our descent suddenly ceased and we began to ascend that one could breathe comfortably. Leafage appeared over the last hill and we soon reached our goal, a garden of luxuriant vegetation, topped with cork, chestnut, and oak trees, brought to life by a boisterous little stream of exquisitely pure water.

We paid our respects to two elderly gentlewomen, sisters of a dead canon, and

The Morena

drank slowly at the spring situated before the door of their stone cottage, their hired men coming and remaining to silently gaze upon us till we resumed our march.

Following the stream through the gardens, crossing and recrossing it, jumping over mud walls, stooping low under pear- and apple-trees, we came at last upon a family of children taking a bath under the watchful eyes of the mother. A little naked boy, frightened at our appearance, burst out crying and calling "Mamma," while his little girl companions laughed at him and at us.

The contents of the cart were unloaded in a secluded spot on the edge of the oasis. The members of our party set about busily getting wood and water, and putting wine and vegetables to cool in a deep pool. When the fire was lit, if someone wandered away, it was only for a moment, soon returning to resume his patient watch before the frying-pan, over which Doña Teresa presided. Pathetic spectacle—this fascination food exerts over these people, for it means simply that they have not often a chance to do full justice to their appetites. They are like the Arabs, who, living on the most frugal and

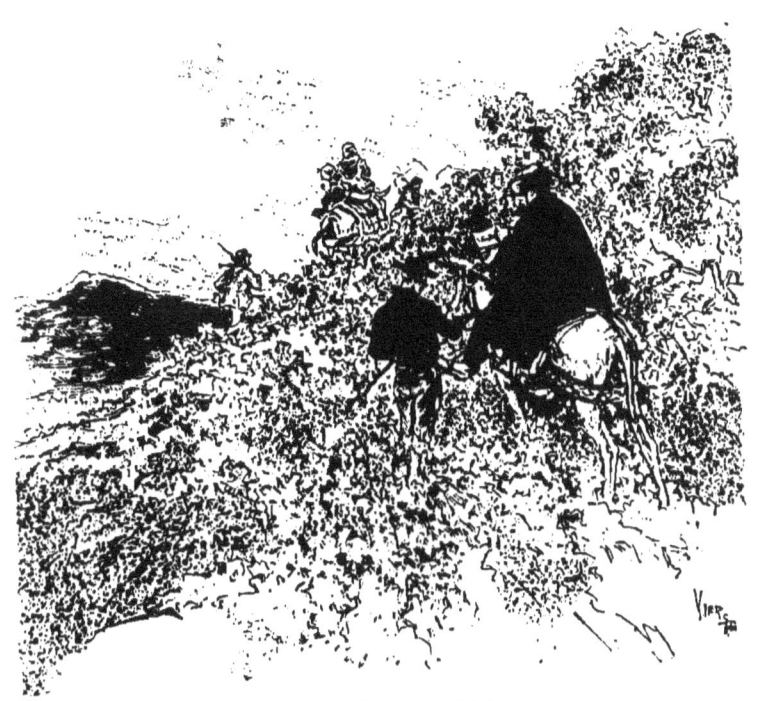

On the Road to Los Molinos.

The Morena

scanty diet, whenever opportunity offers, have their revenge and gorge themselves to the verge of stupor.

We had a jolly time discussing the elaborate repast, Teresa's flow of unexpected sallies making the eyes of the Guardias bulge out comically, and interfering with the attention they gave to the business of filling up.

"Take care, honey, wine makes the whiskers grow and the beaux fly," she remarked to the girl-servant about to take wine, and who

protested that she was not covetous, and did not care a wild fig for any beaux. Teresa quoted: "He that lies most will sin most"

The Morena

(*Quien mas miente, medra mas*), an old proverb which was chosen by Quevedo as the title of one of his plays; and winked at her husband, " in faith she'll have dozens of them. I keep my eye on her, but what's the good, 'my mother beats me and I whip the toys'" (*Castigame mi madre y yo trompógelas*), one of Quevedo's proverbs which, applied here, means I chastise her but she continues to play her game. To which the child answered, sotto-voce, "It's not my fault, anyhow. '*No con quien naces sino con quien paces.*' Not with whom thou art bred but with whom thou art fed."

The eatables disposed of, the wine-skins empty, even the gallon of salad mixture— equal parts of vinegar and water in which tomatoes, cucumbers, and onions had swum —drunk and relished, the only possible outcome of this gastronomic debauchery in such a place was the immediate siesta in which all indulged.

On waking I saw my companions strewn about sound asleep in the shade, their arms under their flushed cheeks. Near the cart the gaunt old mule was munching her fodder, her ribbed anatomy brought out by light and

On the Road to Los Molinos.

The Morena

shadow. At the foot of the meadow the little servant-girl hummed softly to herself. Bud of a potential coquette she was rehearsing her artful feminine tricks, tilting her head, making a pretence to courtesy, and essaying some particularly fetching dance figure.

A grove of tall chestnuts and pines on the edge of the meadow encircled the square stone basin where the precious benefactor of the gardens had its source. From its bottom of sand and pebbles there rose through the clear crystal continuous strings of bubbles. Fish swam in and out of the moss which clothed the stone and floated on the surface of the water, and dragon-flies and swallows, darting in rapid zigzags, snatched a tiny drink.

The deep silence was broken by the spasmodic, harmonious tinkling of the mule-bells and the far-away trill of a solitary song-bird. The wind, gathering strength as it approached, like waves galloping to the shore, came in recurrent gusts with long rustlings agitating the tree-tops. Between the tree-trunks, apparently near enough to touch, our big neighbors, the enormous cliffs, blazed in the flam-

boyant light which revealed the strangely colored veins running through their precipitous declivities, and all their wealth of picturesque and rugged beauty. In a like place the knight performed his self-imposed penance "at the foot of a lofty mountain" along the skirt of which ran "a gentle streamlet" encircling "a green and luxuriant meadow." It may be the very spot Cervantes had in mind, although the consensus of learned opinion has placed it a few leagues farther east. The impression made by this happy and peaceful little world, with its running water

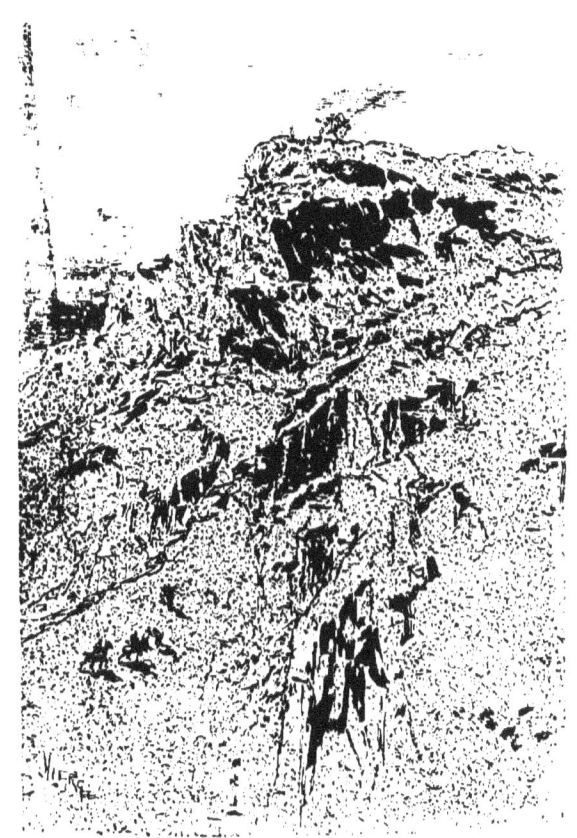

The Pia del Panero.

and luxuriance of vegetation in the midst of the most forbidding scenery, was like that of an oasis in the limitless sands of the Sahara.

We started late for El Viso. The sun was burning, yet long before reaching the hospitable Casa Teresa we wrapped ourselves in overcoats and blankets, the transition at sunset being so abrupt from heat to cold.

I went to Los Molinos alone with my couple of Guardias, it being far too hard an excursion for the Señora and her husband—taking one as it did into "the very bowels of the mountain," in the midst of such wild scenery as Cervantes described in those chapters wherein are recounted the knight's adventures with the Tattered One, Cardenio.

This deserted, trackless maze of rough hills and valleys, inaccessible except to men who know the ground well, was in old days the refuge of those who sought escape from justice and from the Inquisition, and until the last generation they were the haunts of bands of brigands, whose bloody exploits remaining vividly impressed upon the popular imagina-

The Morena

tion, are still on the lips of men, women, and children in the region.

It took us fourteen hours of the hardest walking to get to the mill, which, in spite of the dangerous path connecting it with the rest of the world, is not altogether abandoned. Water-power is scarce, fuel too expensive, and so with serious risks of losing mules or sacks of flour on the way, this mill, whose fine water-power can turn out flour cheaply, is perforce patronized by the poorer folks alone, and kept going a few months of the year.

Not only is the way dangerous for beasts, but it is not without perils for the pedestrian. The shiny, smooth rock or the loose, broken stones on the steep descents offering an equally uncertain footing, may easily be the means of landing him at the bottom of a precipice. The path is staked out with heaps of stones, perpetuating the memory of such accidents, and to each of these, following the custom, we religiously added a stone in passing. This custom is still enforced nowadays in Sicily and in the whole of Northern Africa.

But the scenery was grand in the ex-

The Morena

treme. Titanic crags alternated with groves of robust myrtles and lentisks, with slopes where the trailing arbutus and laurels grew in profusion above carpets of daisies and carnations in the valleys whose air was pungent with penetrating aromas. We found out the truth of the proverb (*no hay atajo sin trabajo*) "there is no short cut without hard work" in the last part of the journey, which we made jumping from boulder to boulder, after the fashion of Cardenio, the One Crazed by Love. It was the only way to reach our destination quickly, and as safe a one as the mule-path.

Set at the bottom of a narrow pit, surrounded on all sides with almost perpendicular giant walls that seemed about to crush it, was the mill, the most forlorn, miserable place I had as yet seen. Untenanted at the time, it stared at us from its windowless apertures like a corpse from eyeless sockets. Behind its rotten door we found, tenanted by bats and rats, a dirty room whose vast, musty emptiness, framed by tottering walls, produced a tragic and forlorn impression. There was no relief in anything. All was abjectly sordid—hopeless. The water was icy cold

The Morena

and so was the night. We built a fire in the middle of the floor and slept by it, each one of us keeping watch in turn.

When I arrived at El Viso the next night, thoroughly exhausted, I felt as if I had been through one of the circles of the Inferno.

VII

Venta de Cardenas

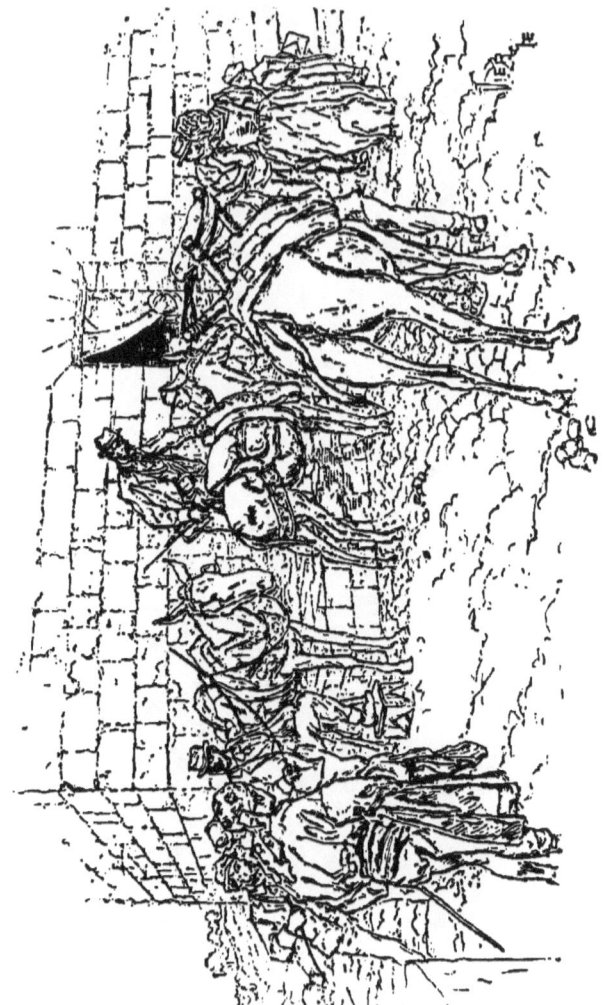

A Start in the Morena.

Venta de Cardenas

I LEFT Viso with José and his cart and two Guardias in the middle of one of those starry nights when the atmosphere is diaphanous and a warm wind, velvety and caressing, makes travelling an unadulterated pleasure, even if the prospects for the coming day are fraught with the probabilities of a thunder-storm.

After a league or more I found myself on the same Royal Highway connecting Madrid with Seville that had led me formerly toward Toboso. We followed it southward where the divers groups of the Sierra summits were distributed about us in an architectural confusion full of striking character that changed alluringly with the direction, the ascents and descents of the road.

A few ruins alone remain to tell of the ancient prosperity and busy life of this great thoroughfare, whose solid construction still defies the elements. We called for a cup of coffee at the ruins of a Venta where, in the two rooms still intact lived a young couple, the man surly, the woman with the look of a beaten hound, both with manners strangely constrained that made us silent and uncomfortable. The Guardias explained, when we were on our way again, how the husband was jealous of his wife, and that was why they lived in such a wilderness, miles away from any human being.

At the lowest point of a long descent the road turned abruptly to the right, crossing a bridge thrown over a rapid torrent. Facing the bridge and tumbling down hill was an avalanche of gigantic bowlders, the road turning from them straight down and following the other side of the torrent, which it recrossed at another bridge a hundred yards below. These bowlders, commanding the road, long stretches of which were visible above and below, afford an ideal place for brigands to lie in ambush. And in this place more murders and robberies have been committed than in all the rest of Spain, so my Guardias said. Until the introduction of the Remington and Martini-Henry rifles, mules and loads were stolen, coaches held up, and when travellers refused to surrender or made

Venta de Cardenas

a show of resistance they were butchered and their heads cut off and set on the parapet of the bridge to serve as a warning.

On one of the summits to the right of the road, the cavern of the Paolos, head-quarters of a renowned band, was visible. The Paolos were brothers in blood and crime whose exploits were among the choicest bogy tales with which José, who had seen one of the Paolos, regaled me. They were grewsome and revolting stories.

Thanks mainly to the efficient work of the Guardia Civile the road is now absolutely safe from brigands, and has been for long, yet when I questioned my men as to what possible dangers there could be for me in travelling alone about here, they said that there would be none for poor people, but that some rough, ignorant chap of an *arriero* who happened to cross my path might take a notion to put his steel into me on the chance of finding a peseta or something better on my person. The amusing thing about it was, that with my scanty and poor Manchegan habiliments I had imagined myself an ideal picture of a penniless tramp.

The road continued to skirt the waterway,

Venta de Cardenas

which, losing its wildness, had now become a gently bubbling little river. The railroad overtaking it passed over it, and with river and railroad for constant company we kept on steadily down grade, meeting not a soul. No trains passed, and the noise of the waters was the only voice breaking the oppressive stillness.

The mountains gradually crowded upon us and towered high with their garments of

Venta de Cardenas

woods, pierced through in places by prismatic excrescences of rock. Our path was strewn with falling débris, constantly disintegrated from the rocks by the action of the elements. Rich, metallic chunks of quartz showed the wealth lying fallow in these Morena Mountains, celebrated even in the days of the Roman occupation for mines of copper, lead, antimony, and silver which have been abandoned or forgotten for centuries.

Venta de Cardenas

Before the lonely station of Venta de Cardenas we came upon the most miserable settlement of any on my travels. A half-dozen low, windowless, mud hovels, wallowed in pools of filth where pigs rooted and chickens waded. Repulsive specimens of humanity, in vile rags and tatters, and dirty beyond imagining, slouched in doorways, regarding us with stupid stares. One felt that any moment they might go down on all-fours and grovel with the animals from which they seemed so slightly removed.

How these beings can continue so low in

Venta de Cardenas

the human scale in a country where the land could, with labor, be made to bear decent returns is a puzzling question, unless one considers the answer to be the ownership of the mountains by rich proprietors who are keeping them as game preserves.

These peasants have no resource but poaching. Too ignorant to know how to send the game they kill to the cities by rail, and unable to dispose of it in the miserable villages of the region, they simply kill in order to support life, and their existence, passed between eating, sleeping, and outwitting the gamekeepers, is as primitive and degraded as that of their ancestors of the Flint Age.

Beyond the station the road climbs the flanks of the ever-narrowing valley, having as protection on the side of the precipice a chaplet of *moriones*, the stone posts set up every few yards of the way, which were so typical and picturesque a feature of old Spanish roads. These *moriones* point the way to the Venta de Cardenas, situated near the entrance to the celebrated cañon of Despeñaperros. It is there that the luxuriant growth of the cactus begins heralding Andalusia, whose very name is music; the land

Venta de Cardenas

of castanets and flowers, of bewitching *cigar-reras* and dancing girls, of gitanos and toreadors, and all sorts of folk equally fascinating in romance and commonplace in reality.

Of old the life of the Morena centred about this defile of Despeñaperros, literally meaning, "thrown-over dogs," probably signifying that here was seen the last of those infidel hounds, the Moors, when, abandoning Toledo and their northern province,

they retreated toward Andalusia. Despeñaperros remained the dividing-line between Christians and Moors during the latter's oc-

Venta de Cardenas

cupation of Grenada. It was then the true Portal of the South, through which passed all the traffic between the capital, Seville, and Andalusia; but in place of the animation of old days, the strings of coaches and troops of loaded mules, there are, but a few times a day, the screeching whistle and rumbling noise of a railway train. It is still the gate of Andalusia, but its life has vanished, and it is probably more lonely now than it

Night Scene at the Venta de Cardenas.

Venta de Cardenas

has been at any time since the Romans conquered Iberia.

The Venta de Cardenas, precious relic of the times when travelling was done by carriages or on foot, looks down upon the only new feature of the scene, its enemy, the railroad. What a brilliant, active, well-filled life the old caravansary has had ! How many historical figures—kings and queens, princes of the Church and ambassadors, captains and merchants from the Indies—have stopped within its walls, elbow to elbow with the common fray, the muleteers, and soldiers. It remains substantially as it was built over three centuries ago, solid, though neglected and telling its pathetic story in its old stones, enormous stables, and big gateway, large enough for two royal carriages to pass through.

We had a noonday feast in the grand old place. The *ama*, a fine type of *Maritórnes*, deigned to do the cooking. (True, there were no servants.) The place had a fine air, and pigeons, and chickens, cats and swallows, filled its lofty emptiness with some sort of life. In the enormous room where we walked about and lay down to rest,

Venta de Cardenas

which is hall, dining-room, and carriage-house combined, a hundred of our carts could have moved about easily.

When our little party sat before the low bench, over which a couple of partridges and a rabbit made a brave show side by side with the palatable salad of cucumbers and tomatoes swimming in a big bowl of vinegar and water, we all dipped our spoons democratically into the dish, while cats and chick-

Venta de Cardenas

ens, trooping around, begged, each after his fashion, and not being gratified, attempted to steal.

Two miserable fellows in scanty attire of shirt and trousers, and those not whole, and with scarlet kerchiefs tied on their heads, came in with the defiant alertness of true Bohemians. They did not succeed in disguising their half-rowdy, half-gypsy looks even before

the Guardias. Having saluted every one with a word, they sat down by the wall opposite us, depositing with extreme care a bundle of rags, from which emerged a straight sword, carefully wrapped up. "*Toreros*," José said. One was no more, evidently, than an acolyte, some apprenticed *banderillero*, probably ; the other—the *espada*—had a strikingly handsome face, yet with a sinister hint of the devil upon it. A lithe and muscular figure, he stood against the wall as gracefully poised as a Greek statue. He asked a few questions, answered charily by our guards, who put on an official attitude of disapprobation. The strangers were Andalusians going to the province of Ciudad Real (La Mancha) to see if they could find out when and where the little local bull-fights took place.

They were blissfully ignorant of the fact that this was the province of Ciudad Real. Apparently they thought of nothing besides the artful tricks of the *torero*, and how to attain such proficiency in them as to become celebrated, wear good clothes, travel in state, and have their fill of the best. Looking like famished beings or feline beasts of prey, with noiseless and nimble gestures, a foxy look in their eyes, they would not give up their hope of being invited to join us till the last chance was gone. The *amo*, *ama*, and the children followed us at table, and there was nothing

In a Popular Resort of Seville.

Venta de Cardenas

left when they finished. So I gave the toreros a small silver coin. Judging from their surprised expression it must have been the first they had ever received in this way. The smiles told plainly that they were not sure but there was something the matter with the giver's wits. But they took it and treasured it in many folds of a rag, and I was convinced that when it should leave its possessors it would be for more than an ordinarily full compensation.

As we stood by the gateway another typical group of barefooted travellers made its appearance. A woman sitting on the top of a load on a donkey's back, her husband leading, two children following behind. They belonged to the fakir fraternity, going from village to village, and fiesta to fiesta, selling trinkets, the mother telling fortunes, the boy, the wickedest little fellow I ever saw, making a specialty of the *zapatera*, the Spanish clog dance. Upon the paterfamilias, an ill-humored, villainous-looking scoundrel, our Guardias kept a close watch. Even old José, who had seen "everything," as he used to say, eyed him suspiciously and remarked: "He is of the kind that would cut a fellow's

Venta de Cardenas

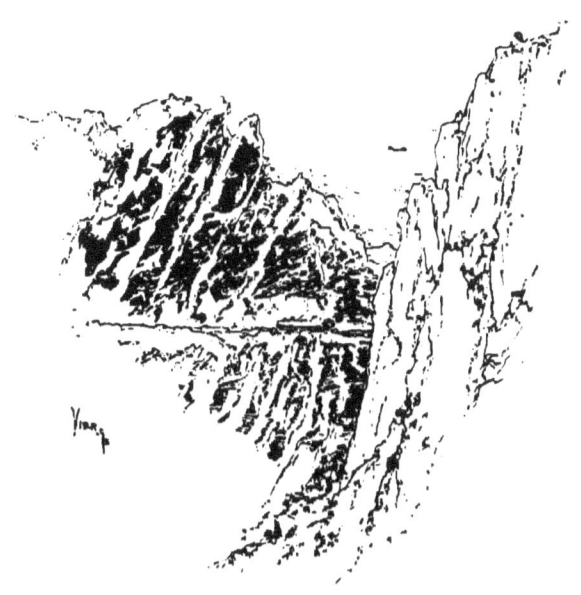

throat just for the fun of the thing." The boy, with an air of bravado sang a fragment of a blasphemous *petenera*:

> I love you more than my life,
> I love you more than my mother;
> And even if it be a sin,
> I love you more than the Virgin of Carmel.

"Shame!" said one of the Guardias. "Don't insult our Lady!" Whereupon the whole party turned and looked at us in feigned surprise.

They spent two cents for the privilege of

Los Organos.

Venta de Cardenas

using the fire to cook something they had brought with them, and for the few hours' shelter for their beast and themselves. They were in vile humor, having fared badly at the fiesta of Viso, and while repacking their donkey's load they gave utterance to their contempt for the Morenans, silly, common, ignorant folk, who would not pay to be amused nor buy good-for-nothing trinkets. However, all was to be well soon, for they were on their way to Seville—" Paradise," they called it. Very like Parisians, these low Sevilians, who think no other town worth living in but their own, and look upon the rest of the world as barbarians.

In the afternoon they trooped out and away toward their beloved goal, the little girl turning somersaults and jumping for joy, the boy imitating the guitar accompaniment to the woman's song :

> Seville of my soul,
> Seville of my joy;
> Who would not love to be in Seville,
> Even though he must sleep on its cobble-stones?

And in the distance the father's rough voice uttered loud, abominable curses at El Viso and the Morenans.

Venta de Cardenas

From the Venta to the end of the great breach of Despeñaperros the Royal Road, narrow and ill-kept, is hewn out of the mountain.

We leisurely followed its smooth curves and sharp turns, each one of which opened a new and impressive vista. On our right the bare walls towered straight up into the blue vault amid the fleecy cloudlets. On our left was the precipice; half-way down its side the railroad, ribbon-like, passed over bridges and occasionally disappeared into tunnels, and at the bottom, two thousand feet below, the greenish boiling waters hurried on toward the Guadalquivir and Andalusia. The thick groves of wild olives and scrubby oaks on the declivities; the luxuriance of ferns, creeping plants, and vivid grass, studded with flowers below; the rigid barrenness of the enormous masses of stone, composed a finely dramatic ensemble. Some of the scenes each turn of the road revealed may have been more picturesque than others —the finest was perhaps that of *Los Organos*, a piece of sheer rock four thousand feet high, whose regular ridges give it a vague resemblance to a row of gigantic organ-pipes—but

Malagueña.

Venta de Cardenas

the whole cañon offered an ever-varying succession of grandiose and superb scenery.

The sun disappeared from our view, and during the rest of our tramp through the passage, darkness and dampness reigned absolute and all its beauties were obliterated.

When we emerged at last from the gloom, there was framed between the two sentinels of Despeñaperros, looming up black and forbidding, a splendid vision of Andalusia. Its denuded hills were transfigured into a medley of incandescent glowing hues looking like the heart of a volcano—under a glorious sky of melted gold, which gradually faded and changed into opal. Later the mirage became something mysterious and indefinable, cradled for the night under a veil of transparent softness.

On coming back the moon had begun shedding its weird radiance over the gorge, evoking a fantastic world of shadows and lights. An *arriero* passed us seated sidewise atop his donkey and vociferating a wild *malagueña* which he accompanied on his guitar.

"Brother," said one of the Guardias, "where art thou going?"

"Home, man," he replied at the top of his voice; "I am going home! Viva la gracia. Que bella! Que guapa! Andalusia!"

www.ingramcontent.com/pod-product-compliance
Lightning Source LLC
Chambersburg PA
CBHW032149230426
43672CB00011B/2495